FREUD
SOME LITERARY PERSEPCTIVES

FREUD

SOME LITERARY PERSPECTIVES

DAVID GORDON

with an afterthought by
Camelia Elias

EyeCorner Press

© DAVID GORDON & EyeCorner Press | 2014

FREUD: SOME LITERARY PERSPECTIVES

Published by EYECORNER PRESS
November 2014

ISBN: 978-87-92633-35-4

Cover design and layout:
Camelia Elias

Collage based on Freud posing for sculptor Oscar Nemon in Vienna, 1931. Photo credit: AP / Wide World Photos

Printed in the UK and US

CONTENTS

The Comic Element in Freud's Tragic Vision / 7

Harold Bloom Reads Freud / 14

On the Difficulty of Understanding Darwin and Freud / 29

When Novelists Compete with Freud:
Lawrence, Murdoch, Robinson / 35

Memory in Proust and Cognitive Neuroscience / 45

Imagining One's Own Death: Freud and the Poets / 59

Reformulating Freud's Hamlet / 67

Georg Brandes and Sigmund Freud: Good Europeans / 82

The Value of Psychoanalysis Today (2014) / 91

§

Singular Time: Three Freudian Essentials
by Camelia Elias / 97

About the Essays

Sorting through papers accumulated during recent years of academic retirement, I found a number of essays testifying to my abiding fascination with Freudian psychoanalysis as well as with literature, the substance of my career. I have selected nine of these, which touch on a range of topics but reflect a recurrent set of concerns and may be effectively grouped together.

About half of these essays were informally presented at annual conferences of the Institute for the Psychological Study of the Arts (IPSA). One of them, "Reformulating Freud's Hamlet," is an extensive revision of a paper published in a 2009 volume called Psychoanalytic Encounters: Interdisciplinary Papers in Applied Psychoanalysis, put together by the Faculty of Philosophy at the University of Belgrade. None of the others has been previously published.

The Comic Element in Freud's Tragic Vision

The cornerstone of Freud's tragic vision is his perception of the ego's inevitable vulnerability. This ego is beset from within as well as without, and whatever unity it manages to achieve in the course of development is bound to be unstable because of interference from the mental underworld. Lucky individuals grow up with fewer problems, and everyone finds forms of gratification to soften frustration, but inner conflict cannot be avoided because it originated in early childhood when the ego was undeveloped and had to deal with it by the inefficient means of repression, which causes (or, by a later theory, results from) anxieties belonging to the infantile situation.

Freud retained this basic picture of individual fate, but broadened it in the course of his career to include the frustrations arising from social arrangements, declaring "Our civilization imposes an almost intolerable burden on us and it calls for a corrective." He directed pungent barbs at unenlightened social arrangements, but did not have enough trust in governments to seek political solutions. The frustrations he emphasized derived from the nature of things, from what he liked to call Reality or, using an impressive Greek word meaning Necessity, *Ananke*. From *Totem and Taboo* (1912) to *Moses and Monotheism* (1938), he boldly sought to discover the original source of our trouble in prehistory, in the ancient crime of parricide and its consequence of guilt. This slide from history into myth has been criticized, but Freud supported the hypothesis by expanding psychoanalytic theory in a way that won broad approval. In works ranging from "On Narcissism" (1914) to *The Ego and the Id* (1923) he developed the concept of a superego, which entailed cultural as well as paternal prohibition, and thus widened the scope of unconscious determination, which now included not only the id but the superego and even much of the ego. Our imperfect efforts to resolve infantile conflicts, he concluded, must result in a lingering sense of loss and guilt, of unhappiness.

Such, in outline, is the familiar picture of Freud's tragic vision. But it does not capture at all well the spirit of the psychoanalysis he created, which is not only committed as a therapy to *relieving* unhappiness but is animated at every point by the spirit of *comedy*.

There are, we may say as literary critics, two basic forms of comedy. One, Type A, is generated by incongruity and discordance, typically arousing in a audience amusement, surprise or embarrassment. Accordingly, the three treatises that launched Freud's psychoanalytic career – on dreams, jokes and mistakes – analyze these primary elements of Type A comedy. (I have sometimes thought that a comprehensive study of Shakespearean comedy could be organized around precisely these topics.) The second form of comedy, Type B, elevates the ego above the problems it confronts, and is implied in Freud's 1928 essay "On Humor." It might be described as romantic or heroic because it is generated by stories of the ego's invulnerability or invincibility, its ability to triumph over difficulties. Examples range from popular tales of superheroes at one end to the supremely serious instance at the other of Dante's *Commedia* in which the first-person narrator passes arduously but successfully through Inferno and Purgatorio into Paradiso.

Incongruity in Type A comedy arises from a gap between our initial judgment that something is senseless and a later, corrected judgment. The manifest dream seems at first nonsense, the joke at first absurd, the mistake or slip at first illogical. And these are not sideline concerns in the psychoanalytic scheme of things but phenomena that call into play its essential interpretative strategies. In clinical encounters, analyst and patient confront again and again the discovery of a gap between what is said and what is meant, between a questionable surface meaning and a hidden meaning that renders what is said more intelligible. The filling in of emotively significant and inherently comic gaps is pretty much what psychoanalytic therapy is all about. Consider the transference, said to play a crucial role in the interview. A patient is told with some emphasis but cannot quite believe that he or she is confusing the familiar analyst with someone else, a situation fairly characterized by Jacques Lacan as belonging to theatrical farce. The gaps involved in jokes and slips are, of course, not difficult to interpret. The joke possesses a social dimension, requiring two parties who share the pleasure of completing the sense. And the slip, though it may well cause embarrassment, can often be interpreted by the person who makes it, without outside help. But the elusive dream poses a more difficult and rewarding challenge to interpretation and was accordingly described by Freud as "the royal road to the unconscious."

Type B comedy, in which, rather than being humbled, the ego triumphs over difficulties, may seem incidental to psychoanalysis but is in fact essentially characteristic of Freud's mode of self-presentation, his rhetorical stance as a writer. From his university days on, Freud identified himself with the mythic figure of Oedipus, not the tragic but the triumphant Oedipus who solved the riddle of the sphinx and whose modern incarnation could explain the haunting power of a tragic story *about* unwitting incest and parricide. Freud too, without tragic consequence, will track down an ancient psychological crime, bringing all to light as interpreter. This identification lasted throughout his life. In old age, he sometimes referred to his beloved and useful daughter Anna as his Antigone.

Typically, Freud sets up a piece of writing as a challenging problem to be solved, dramatizing the process of interpretation. Consider "Dora: An Analysis of a Case of Hysteria," an essay faulted by some for showing his insensitivity to the age, sex and situation of his patient. What is seldom noticed is the way Freud, in his eagerness to solve the riddle of hysteria, casts Dora as an *ally* in an heroic enterprise. The task of bringing to light what human beings keep hidden, he writes, is "*with her help* proving easier than I first supposed" (my italics). Consider again his choice of epigraph for the monumental treatise *The Interpretation of Dreams*: "*Flectere si nequeo superos, Acheronta movebo*" (If I cannot bend the higher powers, I will bend the infernal regions). Critics have imputed Promethean pride to Freud for his choice of this Virgilian verse, associating the "I" with the writer rather than, as intended, with the mind's unconscious urgency, symbolized by the will of the goddess. We understand Freud's protest against this imputation, but ambiguity remains because his ambition throughout this long treatise is on so grand a scale. One more example of his heroic persona is the quotable formula for the overall objective of psychoanalysis: *Wo Es war, soll Ich werden,* translated by Strachey in the Standard Edition as "Where Id was, there Ego shall be." This was far too ego-idealizing for Lacan, whose own clever translation, reversing the order and thus the sense of the German phrases, can be rendered: "*I must come to the place where It was.*" But Freud's own follow-up, "It is reclamation work, like the draining of the Zuyder Zee," would suggest to German speakers the high-minded ambition of Goethe's Faust and thus support the Strachey translation.

This heroic/romantic type of comedy should not be confused with the kind of fantasy represented by daydreaming. Critics have rightly objected to Freud's oversimplified accounts of the creative process in his 1908 essay "Creative Writers and Daydreaming" and again in the 1911 essay "On the Two Principles of Mental Functioning," essays in which he describes the artist as a man who turns away from reality but finds a way back through shared fantasy. Freud himself achieves a more subtle understanding when he engages serious rather than merely popular works – in, for example, "The Theme of the Three Caskets," "The Moses of Michelangelo," and "The Uncanny." In the first of these essays, he shows that Bassanio's surprising choice of the lead over the gold and silver casket entails the hidden presence of death; in the second, Moses in the famous sculpture represents the high mental achievement of struggling successfully against an inward passion for the sake of a worthy cause; and in "The Uncanny" he demonstrates that the effect of Hoffmann's story crucially depends upon the role of judgment, judgment serving precisely to *distinguish* reality from fantasy.

The heroic stance implied in Freud's writing was associated as a rule with the work of the "scientist" rather than the work of the "poet." But his *oeuvre* surely ranks as *mythopoesis* as well as psychological science because its grand narrative of human development altered a whole culture's understanding of itself, much as did Darwin's evolutionary and Marx's economic grand narratives. "The distinctive contribution of such writers," wrote Michel Foucault," is that they produced not only their own work but the endless possibility of other texts." And it is the rhetoric of Freud's self-presentation that opens up this larger possibility. We are drawn to this writer's heroic defiance of public opinion, whether the subject is the boldness of a message concerning sexuality, the isolation endured as a result of that message, the defection of followers or the strain of being Jewish in anti-Semitic Vienna. The pride of the writer in these cases is something different from the *hubris* of a tragic hero. When Freud describes himself as someone who has disturbed the world's sleep, the language is neither boastful nor regretful, merely an acknowledgment of a likely influence that posterity will have to deal with as it sees fit.

The English Romantic essayist Thomas De Quincey distinguished between a literature of knowledge and a literature of power. The writings of Freud belong to both and often inseparably. But its status as a literature of power needs more definition than it has received. De Quincey's phrase alerts us to an important paradoxical fact about great writers in general: no matter how dark, how pessimistic their view of the world, they cannot fail to be *celebrants* as well as pessimists because they cannot help sharing with their readers their delight in their own strength. My favorite thumbnail characterization of Freud comes from the literary critic Harold Bloom, who links him with Marcel Proust. The two writers in Bloom's nice phrasing are "tragic celebrants of the comic spirit."

Examining Freud through a literary rather than a scientific lens helps to answer two persistent questions concerning his reputation. One is, why does it seem both right and wrong to describe him as a scientist? And the other, why, in spite of the fact that psychoanalysis has lost prestige over the last half century, does the Freudian presence continue to exert so much fascination and the Freudian narrative continue to carry so much weight?

Harold Bloom Reads Freud

From 1970 to the present, the prolific and impassioned literary criticism of Harold Bloom has been rife with commentary on Sigmund Freud's psychoanalytic theory of mind. The commentary is always combative, and promotes an intellectual battle in which the White Knight of Poetry resourcefully outmaneuvers, although he cannot quite defeat, the Dark Knight of Psychoanalysis. The battle has developed, we can see now, in two phases. In an energetic first phrase occupying the 1970s, Bloom sought chiefly to undermine and even co-opt key terms in the psychoanalyst's vocabulary, especially repression. In a second phase, extending from the late 1980s into the new century, he has, somewhat grudgingly, welcomed Freud the writer into the literary pantheon as a "superb" (or at any rate "inevitable") moral essayist. Charting this contest can clarify the strengths and vulnerabilities of two brilliant thinkers who as writers, I will indicate finally, have traits in common.

"The Internalization of Quest Romance," an essay published in journal form in 1968 and as part of a book (*The Ringers in the Tower*) in 1971, opens Bloom's long and complex struggle with Freud. Its initial move is to establish the English Romantic poets as authentic psychologists in that they relocated the setting of traditional quest romances from an external world to the mind itself. Thus the *subject* of their major poems becomes *subjectivity itself*. They typically confront and put to use anxieties that could inhibit imaginative flight, hoping thereby to widen their sense of imaginative freedom, a project initiated by their chief forerunner, John Milton, who sought on behalf of Adam and Eve "a paradise within thee, happier far."

This observation leads Bloom to what the essay is mainly about, the contrast between the expansive, sometimes even apocalyptic humanism of Romantic psychology (represented chiefly by Blake, Wordsworth and Shelley) and the naturalistic humanism of Freudian psychology. He sees the Romantic quest, unlike Freud's, as not limited by the almighty Reality Principle ("the ugliest of Muses"), which teaches the wisdom of working out compromises that recognize Necessity (and its ultimate form, death) rather than abiding by the promise of what Wordsworth called "something evermore about to be." What is it, Bloom asks challengingly, that resists enchantment? Is it in truth a Reality Principle or only anxiety masquerading as reality? Freud teaches self-knowledge, but isn't this (again in Wordsworthian phrasing) "knowledge purchased by the loss of power"?

Choosing between Freudian and Romantic psychology depends for Bloom on whether we think of the human mind as permanently scarred by childhood and trying to work out some accommodation for itself or whether we think of the mind in its creative strength as capable of renovating consciousness, achieving something like a second birth, and thus attaining a revenge against time, against mortality itself. Bloom likes to illustrate this strength in the "crisis poems" of the great Romantics, occasions when the imagination appears to be stalled by fear and anxiety but then proves able, through the power of inventive language, to liberate itself.

The essay devotes some attention to the contrasting theories of love found in these two psychologies. Attempting to appreciate Freud's humane wisdom, Bloom admires his "beautiful sentence: A man shall leave father and mother – according to the biblical precept – and cleave unto his wife; thus are tenderness and sensuality united." But he soon finds this idea flawed because it means that what essentially characterizes the course of human love is entropy, a progressive loss of satisfaction. The critic's language becomes sarcastic: "it is better thus, as there is no satisfaction in satisfaction anyway, since in the Freudian view all erotic partners are somewhat inadequate replacements for the initial sexual objects." He even wonders, with reference to Freud's text "On Narcissism," whether we are to conclude that *self-love* is better anyway – in contrast to the poets who warned against the danger of solipsism, like Shelley with his Alastor and Blake with his Spectre.

Trying in this early essay to offset what he recognizes as a prejudicial view of psychoanalytic teaching about affective influence, Bloom resourcefully finds a parallel between Freud and the Romantics. The Freudian idea of growth by transferring love from parent to spouse is, after all, similar to what the strong Romantic poet must do imaginatively: he must "leave" (Bloom would soon prefer to say "repress") the influence of his strong poetic predecessor or "parent" and discover his own originality through creative competition. With this parallel, the critic is clearly looking ahead to the theory soon to be formulated in his *Anxiety of Influence*, a watershed moment in his own intellectual development.

The years 1973-1976 saw the publication of three books (*The Anxiety of Influence*, *A Map of Misreading* and *Poetry and Repression: Revisionism from Blake to Stevens*) that established Bloom's credentials as a major critic. The last two in particular launch a still bolder critique of Freud. They skeptically dig into crucial concepts for a psychoanalytic theory of mind – defense, drive, and repression – and into the concept of unconscious mental process that anchors them all.

In *The Map of Misreading* Bloom takes aim at what he calls the Freudian "reductiveness," the way psychoanalytic theory adopts a literal rather than metaphorical understanding of its key concepts. Whereas for Freud the word psyche or mind is understood as the seat of interacting drives and defenses, Bloom understands mind as, above all, the seat of figuration. Accordingly, he proposes another mode of interpretation based on an advanced theory of poetry. After all, Freud had derived the very idea of an unconscious mind from the poets or, one might say, "from Schopenhauer and Nietzsche who themselves had taken it from the poets." There is, for Bloom, no deepest layer of the mind, no unconscious beyond what the *poet* represses, and the anxiety that the poet represses *energizes invention*, stimulates brilliant rhetorical hyperbole for which the critic's favorite label is The Sublime.

In the twenty-seven dense pages of introduction to *Poetry and Repression: Revisionism from Blake to Stevens*, Bloom caps this idea by arguing that the anxiety of most concern to the poet derives from the strength of an influential precursor. A strong poet's chief concern is to gain a conviction, albeit illusive, of poetic priority. To do so he must demonize or "repress" the precursor's poem. Bloom co-opts the Freudian term repression to describe important *imaginative* action as it occurs in the psychic battlefield he most values. He ignores the infantile mind and thus the battlefield delineated in Freud's developmental account of man where the influence of parents rather than poets looms so large. More exactly, he co-opts the parental role, converting biological parents into poetic precursors. The influential precursor poet becomes a "father figure" whose example burdens his would-be rival with a crippling sense of belatedness. In response, a strong poet seeks to *become the father of his father.* Literally impossible, yes, but if his poem is strong, time itself will validate the illusion and thus remake it into truth. This process is basically what Bloom means by revisionism and what he demonstrates to be the case in the subsequent chapters of *Poetry and Repression.*

In the Bloomian overview, Poetry is fighting with Psychoanalysis over the very question of priority. Which comes first, the text (his view) or the psyche (Freud's view). Conventional criticism favors the latter, supposing it is the mind of a person that gets represented by a text. But Bloom argues that a text is primarily *rhetoric* and insists that rhetoric can only be represented or seconded by other rhetoric. If a conventional critic would object that this view ignores the fact that poets are persons and therefore what they write is bound to express what they are as persons, Bloom would, I think, reply that studying the person as a lead-in to the rhetoric weakens the specifically poetic impression and is an invitation to mediocrity.

This brings us to Bloom's curiously heated attack on the psychoanalytic concept of sublimation, a concept hard to understand as a threat to his argument unless it is misunderstood as the cause of a weakened poetic result. In *The Map of Misreading* he writes: "The central argument of this book, as of *The Anxiety of Influence*, is that sublimation is a *defense of limitation*." What this means becomes clearer in *Poetry and Repression*. But to get a handle on it, it is helpful to quote first a satisfactory definition of Freud's term sublimation (I take one from the well-regarded *Language of Psychoanalysis* authored by Laplanche and Pontalis) and put beside it Bloom's scornful view of how the term would be deployed by a hypothetical Freudian critic:

> [*Language of Psychoanalysis*]: Sublimation: Process postulated by Freud to account for human activities which have no apparent connection with sexuality but which are assumed to be motivated by the sexual instinct. The main types of activity described by Freud as sublimated are artistic creation and intellectual inquiry. The instinct is said to be sublimated insofar as it is diverted toward a new non-sexual aim and insofar as its objects are socially valuable ones.
>
> [*Poetry and Repression*] The criticism of poetry that I urge... has nothing in common with 'Freudian literary criticism.' On a strict Freudian view, a good poem is a sublimation, a work of substitution that replaces the gratification of prohibited instincts [causing] flaws in the poem. But poems are actually stronger when their counterintended effects battle most incessantly against their overt intentions.

Bloom understands the term sublimation to mean a process valorized "on supposed resemblances between sexuality and intellectual activity, including poetry." But, as the Laplanche-Pontalis quotation indicates, the term is intended only to account for the transformation of our pervasive libido *with respect to its aims*. It has nothing to do with the merit of a poem, with aesthetic judgment. It is in no sense a substitution. Bloom describes Freud's sublimation as "an underdeveloped and intellectually unsatisfactory notion." "Underdeveloped" it may be, but in this case it is unsatisfactory only because it is misapplied. Bloom seems to be on guard here against poems not strong enough to qualify for his preferred psychodrama, poems that leave personal traces not absorbed by an effective rhetorical action.

I believe this misunderstanding illustrates the collision of contrary analytic approaches. Freud's habitual *evolutionary or genetic* approach stresses how things develop, how the writing of a poem may originate. Bloom's *aesthetic* approach concerns itself with rhetoric, with achieved rhetorical effects. I will return to this fundamental difference between the two modes of analysis.

A subsequent essay titled "Freud's Concept of Repression and the Poetic Will" reads like a follow-up to *Poetry and Repression*. (It appeared as the lead essay in a 1980 volume titled *The Literary Freud: Mechanisms of Defense and the Poetic Will* but had been distributed earlier to contributors responding to it.) In this essay Bloom argues that repression, a process "at the center of Freud's vision of man," must be understood figuratively rather than literally. Are not "flight" and "distancing" tropes after all? And he adds force to the idea by admitting a weakness in his own former argument, for if defenses develop in the child's mind to ward off unacceptable truth and if defenses are tropes, isn't figuration itself as used by poets – isn't the very poetic will that creates metaphor – itself infantile? His corrective view in this essay, bolstered by Shelley and Nietzsche, is that, no matter from what personal anxiety tropes may arise, if they have achieved poetic power, they objectify whatever went into their creation. That is, the poet's *I am thus* becomes *It is thus*. Poetic defense, unlike psychoanalytic defense, is a trope directed at earlier tropes, a successful quest for priority. Bloom instances the way that the successful strong poetry he terms Sublime arises from successful misreading of precursor poems, which is to say from the defense of repression.

This is what may be called the first of two corrective steps in his improved argument on behalf of poetic will. The second concerns a weakness he now perceives in having accepted as a somatic given the Freudian idea of the "drive" that provoked the "defense," for if the drive is understood as a somatic given, it becomes another instance of questionable literalism. Here Bloom's resourceful maneuver is to extend Freud's own idea that the drives are frontier concepts – i.e., both mental and physical – since the ego that initiates the defense is "always a bodily ego" and of course always a psychological category as well. Hence its meaning slides and cannot be restrictively literal. Bloom points out that Freud himself, in his later theoretical revisions, moved toward a more mythic and thus metaphorical understanding of the drives. The sexual drive, newly associated with a concept of primary narcissism, acquires the mythic name of Eros, and the ego drive, newly associated with primary aggression, acquires the mythic name of Thanatos.

From 1980 on, in his adversarial commentary, Bloom welcomes any hint in later Freudian theory that the power and primacy of repression might need to be qualified by a psychic action still more primary – whether it concerns narcissism, aggression or anxiety. Earlier, he claimed that he was taking back for poetry what Freud himself had taken from the poets. Now he begins to suggest that Freud himself may be read (in exemplary tests like "On Narcissism" and *Beyond the Pleasure Principle*) as a poet who is working through a creative crisis that liberates his own stalled imagination. Thus his major revisions in psychoanalytic theory may be read as the effort of his own poetic will to renew the all important quest for priority, a quest so ambitious that it seeks to displace even the stunning originality of his own previous achievements. Bloom had earlier stated, "there is no end to repression in strong poetry," using repression to mean something like the revisionary poetic will. Now this claim includes Freud himself.

This 1980 essay, then, shows a new willingness to modify the view that psychoanalysis is fundamentally incongruous with the poetic will. It suggests that at least the revisionary Freud may be claimed *for* poetry. And in support of this idea Bloom reintroduces with new emphasis a point he had made earlier about Freud's concept of Negation. Freud had proposed that, by the compromise tactic of being "cognitively accepted while affectively denied," a repressed thought or desire makes a partial return from the unconscious to conscious awareness. Bloom would now extend the point, arguing that a mind capable of modifying the determinative repressions of early childhood is doing something not very different from what the strong poetic will can do. But for this extension to develop into a full-blown conviction that Freud may be considered a *literary* figure, a major writer, a few more years had to pass.

I will illustrate the second phase of Bloom's extended response to Freud by means of two essays written a decade or two after those so far discussed: "Freud: A Shakespearean Reading" from *The Western Canon* (1994) and the chapter called "Freud and Proust" from my favorite among his many books, *Where Shall Wisdom Be Found* (2004). The combative tone remains, but there is a significant shift of emphasis. The aim in these essays is not to show that Psychoanalysis is defeated or improved by Poetry but to find a place for Freud *within* the Western canon. This is explicit in the second essay to be considered but is implied, somewhat grudgingly or ironically, in the sassy first essay. We are meant, of course, to be amused by its title. Instead of the conventional phrase, a Freudian reading of writer X, we get the reversal, writer X's reading of Freud. A put-down but with a twist: X in this case is none other than *the* bard, and thus Freud is assigned a literary place – adjunctive, to be sure, but at the topmost rung of this bardolatrous critic's scale of greatness.

Bloom seizes gleefully on the one opinion in Freud's voluminous and controversial work that is frankly ridiculous, his embrace of the speculation that the works of Shakespeare, especially the great tragedies, were written by Edward de Vere, the Earl of Oxford, who died in 1604. It is true that Freud advanced this opinion in footnotes and letters or under cover of anonymity as in "The Moses of Michelangelo" rather than in formal commentary concerning Shakespeare. But this doesn't get him off the hook. He held to it, sometimes irritably, even when rebuked by friends like Ernest Jones and Stefan Zweig.

Bloom convincingly demonstrates that what was at stake for Freud in this misjudgment was the validity of his oedipal interpretation of *Hamlet* and thus of the Oedipus Complex itself, a linchpin of the psychoanalytic theory of human development. With artful phrasing that seems to honor Freud but only because his opinion in this case can be cited as an excellent illustration of a certain kind of newly patented anxiety that he himself had never imagined, Bloom observes that "the anxiety of influence has no more distinguished sufferer in our time than the founder of psychoanalysis.... Shakespeare was the father he could not acknowledge," an interpreter of the human mind who "had been there before him and had to be disgraced" in order to affirm his own priority. A palpable hit.

There are also in this essay some less interesting swipes at Bloom's own rival – Freud's unconscious is "an internal combustion engine"; "Shakespeare was the inventor of psychoanalysis and Freud only the codifier.... a prosified Shakespeare." But by such exaggerated means the oppositional Freud in the first phase of Bloom's attack is gradually altered into a kind of sparring mate, a man with his own vision but an ally in the larger fight on behalf of the republic of letters.

To my mind, none of Bloom's assessments of Freud is so impressive and attractive – so comprehensive and pithy (the two qualities that, combined, distinguish the style of his best literary criticism), as the mere fifteen pages that make up the first half, the Freud half, of the chapter titled "Freud and Proust" in *Where Shall Wisdom Be Found*. In three of these pages, for example, the critic shows convincingly and effortlessly that Jewishness is more central to the achievement of Freud than he cared to believe. A major reason for the essay's success is that Bloom has found, without jeering, a secure place for his rival in the literary pantheon. This anointing of the psychoanalyst as "a superb moral essayist" is stated succinctly on the essay's second page:

> Freud's universal and comprehensive theory of mind will probably outlive the psychoanalytic therapy, and seems already to have placed him with Plato and Montaigne and Shakespeare rather than with the scientists he overtly aspired to emulate.
>
> This is not to suggest that Freud was primarily a philosopher or a poet, but rather that his influence has been analogous to that of Plato, Montaigne and Shakespeare: inescapable, immense, al-

most incalculable....He is at once the principal writer and the principal thinker of our century...unique in that he would dominate the second group and challenge even Proust, Joyce and Kafka in the first.

To be sure, this high praise is accompanied by a grudging element. While noting the impressiveness of "Freud's uncanny stories of our unconscious mental processes," Bloom still doubts the very existence of a repressed unconscious: "What are the motives for such flight?... I find no overt answer to this crucial question in Freud, whose characteristic dualism was too fundamental for questioning." While acknowledging the force of Freud's demonstrations of lasting inner conflict and ambivalence, he yet asks with some irritation, "Why, after all, is the psyche at civil war? What does it war with [causing] the neurotic suffering that robs us of our freedom?" The originator of a theory of poetic influence links Freud's importance to his "pervasive influence" yet resents that influence as well: "As the dead father, Freud is stronger than any living father can be." But, touchingly, we also get a compliment to *this* father figure that reads like an admission of Bloom's *own* anxiety of influence: "our inability to characterize Freud accurately without revising him is a true sign of his greatness."

The grand idea of a renovated consciousness or psychic rebirth has, for Bloom, been evidenced over the years not only by the Romantic tradition but also by the ancient religious tradition of Gnosticism, which endorses the belief that the world we have been given is a false creation and that, by a kind of radical probe of subjectivity, we might discover a new sense of origins. In recent decades Bloom has also shifted some of his interest in literary genius to the American scene: "Emerson," he tells us, "speaks to me directly, even more than Freud." Accordingly, he has found a measure of Emersonian inspiration in what he calls the "American religion," meaning American popular religion as exemplified by Mormonism. Of course Bloom would never exchange his radical sense of individual genius for membership in a church of any kind (any more than Freud would), but his keen interest in these religious ideas of human aspiration has become conspicuous. It is not surprising, then, that when Freudian theory itself touches on the idea of freedom from unconscious determination, as in the essay on Negation, he particularly welcomes the concession.

If there is one idea that runs most consistently through Bloom's shifting attack, it is that Freud's account of inner conflict, with its emphasis on what limits human freedom, does scant justice to our ability at our inspired best to imagine and achieve liberation from such conflict. One fairly obvious problem with this view is that it tends to make an exception only of exceptionally gifted persons. But there is another less obvious problem that is more fundamental in that it suggests a misdirection of the whole attack. Unlike Bloom's aesthetic approach focused on the most advanced and mature forms of civilized accomplishment, Freud's habitual mode of analysis, whether the subject is human development or the higher forms of art, religion and philosophy, is evolutionist and genetic. That is, it understands advanced phenomena by way of their development from more primitive forms. As the psychoanalyst Robert Waelder explained some time ago, in assessing Freud's unsatisfactory view of modern religious belief, this way of thinking unfortunately suggests that the primitive forms of these achievements are *truer* while higher forms have only a kind of derivative existence. Freud, we know, was quite capable of appreciating art, but his way of thinking prevented him from assigning the sort of primary importance to poetry and the poetic will that is so essential for Bloom.

There is, of course, one area of the psychoanalyst's achievement – clinical practice and theory – in which widening the scope of individual inner freedom *does* become a paramount consideration. Bloom pretty much ignores this area, but if Freud is to be judged as a moral philosopher in the tradition of Montaigne and Emerson, then the rationale of psychoanalytic therapy itself acquires a new importance. I am thinking of several writers in recent years, schooled in both psychoanalysis and moral philosophy, who have done exceptionally interesting work in this regard: Jonathan Lear in *Love and Its Place in Nature*, Marcia Cavell in *Becoming a Subject: Reflections in Philosophy and Psychoanalysis*, and Alfred Tauber in *Freud: The Reluctant Philosopher*. Lear and Cavell are themselves clinicians as well as philosophers, and Tauber effectively associates Freud with Spinoza, Kant and Nietzsche as original and potent teachers of psychological growth.

In the last analysis, Bloom's long struggle with Freud reveals a truth that takes us beyond antagonism. It allows us to see that the two writers are profoundly similar when judged as intellectual and rhetorical presences rather than by their specific ideas. Both write with a power of judgment almost uncanny in its immediacy and authority, as if it had come into their possession as a direct gift, unmediated by education. Both write with little or no revision, able apparently to sort out and expound very complex ideas in their minds before putting pen to page. Bloom in a few ways actually identifies with Freud the man and writer, for example when he more than once notes admiringly that Freud wrote up to the end of his long life as he himself clearly has been doing. And he has always had the ability to ignore a writer's ideological biases when what is at issue is the power of his presence as a writer. He has unstintingly admired Samuel Johnson, for example, despite the incompatibility of their political and religious preferences. And he has volubly admired certain modern poets – Yeats, Lawrence, Frost, Stevens – while not failing to notice their unattractively illiberal social opinions.

Summing up, we may make one further observation linking the two antagonistic bodies of work we have been contrasting. The long battle launched by Bloom against Freud leaves the writings of both standing and, indeed, no less formidable than before. One might even argue that each body of work gains strength as a result of its ability to sustain injury from aggressive contact with its rival.

On the Difficulty of Understanding Darwin and Freud

We have grown accustomed to the once shocking idea that Darwin's theory of evolution by natural selection removes divine agency and purpose from the history of life on earth. But we are less comfortable with a further implication of this theory, the idea that the endless changes of life forms have evolved without any agency whatever, that they are only the product of blind processes – random mutations, accidental environmental events – resulting in variation, selection and replication. In the opinion of most biologists today, they are not governed by any purpose pushing in a discernible direction. "Evolution," according to Gerald Edelman, "is unintelligent but very powerful." Its power indeed may be the reason we are sometimes tempted to think of it as purposeful. Even if we overcome this temptation, however, those of us who accept the theory are faced with a peculiar problem. Without either agency or a purposeful progression of events, how can there be an intelligible narrative, and, without an intelligible narrative, how can the theory be explained and understood?

Darwin himself sensed some of this difficulty when he acknowledged that his central idea of natural selection was a metaphor, endowing nature with agency, with the power to select, modify and adapt. He justified this license by remarking blandly that every reader knows what is meant. Darwinists today do much the same. Even tough-minded Richard Dawkins writes dramatically about a "selfish" gene, and excuses himself by assuring us that we can always translate our sloppy language back into respectable terms if we wanted to. (If this could be done so easily, I dare say Dawkins himself would have shown us how.) As for purposeful progression, some find it implied by the fact that, today, species are on average more complex than long ago. But the convincing counter-argument is that any change from what Darwin called "so simple a beginning" would look more complex. Moreover, some species (microbial ones for example) have remained simple while others, like fleas and tapeworms, have evolved into greater *simplicity*.

Attempting to write a satisfactory conclusion to *The Origin of Species*, Darwin could not resist using the phrase "progress towards perfection." His language has prompted Darwinists from T. H. Huxley to the present to caution that successful adaptation does not necessarily entail *moral* progress, that indeed the moral progress fostered by culture requires us sometimes to fight *against* our natural endowment. We know today more clearly than Darwin could that man's big brain is a mixed blessing, inspiring not only remarkable cultural achievements but also the means to destroy life entirely. In the last words of his book, Darwin tries to offer us satisfying closure to the story he has told us: "from so simple a beginning endless forms most beautiful and most wonderful have been and are being evolved." "Beautiful" and "wonderful," however allowably, are exaggerations – what about the emergence of ever new viruses resistant to known medical intervention? And the statement "endless forms... are being evolved" amounts to a tacit admission that, because evolution is ongoing, no closure to the story is possible. Darwin has allowed himself or, to be fair, has been obliged to allow himself, metaphors of agency and purpose, the props of intelligible narrative.

What I have said so far draws on opinion held by representative students of Darwinian theory. My contribution in this little essay will be to show that Freud's explanation of unconscious mental process is similarly dependent on metaphor and narrative to achieve intelligibility. *Every* explanation of an abstract process is, of course, dependent on the shortcut of metaphor to make its meaning intelligible. Otherwise we would be lost in a sea of phenomena like the unforgettable figure of Funes in Borges' tale, "Funes the Memorious." But I want to suggest that the central ideas of Darwin and Freud, natural selection and unconscious determination, are, among scientific theories, peculiarly sensitive in this regard because they pose a greater threat to human self-esteem, shown in part by the fact that they must struggle more than others for general acceptance.

Unconscious processes like evolutionary ones are unintelligent but very powerful, and so we tend to invest them too with agency and purpose, words that evoke a moral frame of reference. We tend to ignore the fact that they cannot be known directly and to accept at face value the metaphorical language required to describe them. Psychoanalytic discourse concerning them, while it usually avoids the metaphor of person or self, has a hard time using the word "ego" without some implication of agency and purpose, concepts that are basic to the study of narrative. We read about this ego as vulnerable and unstable, emerging only gradually in early childhood and too weak during its formation to deal well with powerful desires and fears, and virtually impotent in the state of sleep. We learn that it is subject to regression from such common causes as frustration, fatigue and illness, constantly under pressure from opposing psychological systems that Freud named "id" and "superego." And we remember his capping metaphor, "not master in its own house."

In the major revision of psychoanalytic theory set forth in *The Ego and the Id*, Freud indicated that much of the ego is itself unconscious and is not simply, as earlier postulated, an agency set over against the unconscious. It is not easy to keep in mind that this agency, *Das Ich*, functions so impersonally. It is significant, I think, that popular usage, makes the word "ego" synonymous with vanity or arrogance, oblivious to such complications; a strong ego in common parlance describes an evident weakness of character rather than a hard to understand developmental ability to coordinate conflicting emotions.

What about that other basic constituent of narrative, a progressive account of events? It too is prominent in psychoanalytic literature, which, one could say, began with the case histories recorded in *Studies in Hysteria*. Freud, we remember, ruefully admitted that these histories resembled fictional stories and thus seemed to lack the stamp of serious science. It is fair to say also, as becomes clear in clinical practice, that what happens within persons has much to do with what happens between persons, making the use of narrative indispensable. But analytic literature must proceed by connecting clinical evidence with a theory about an ulterior reality that the evidence supports. This reality itself, unconscious process, is not directly knowable. Hence no dream can be fully interpreted, no analysis can be quite complete. Psychoanalytic therapists tacitly acknowledge this limitation when they explain their insights to patients in the form of inferences, saying you *must have felt*, you *must have believed*.

We sometimes speak glibly of "unconscious emotion." What can that mean? Surely we know what we feel. Surely an affect by its very nature is conscious. In his important 1915 essay "The Unconscious," Freud clarifies this muddled phrase, and leads us to an enlightening distinction. "An emotion," he writes, "is not strictly speaking unconscious, but it may be misconstrued or misunderstood. That is, it consists of two aspects, a conscious idea and an unconscious idea. The two are not, as we suppose, different records of the same content situated in different parts of the mind; nor yet different functional states in the same part; but the conscious idea comprises the concrete idea, the thing, plus the *verbal idea corresponding to it,* whilst the unconscious idea is the thing alone" (my italics). Freud is here anticipating what contemporary neuroscientists like Antonio Damasio and Gerald Edelman are telling us, namely that an idea *begins* as a bodily process and is then translated into verbal form. Thus the use of verbal language, the gift above all that makes us human, sits on top of somatic processes about which whatever can be learned must be expressed through verbal language. The real nature of these processes is unknowable.

This constitutes the fundamental difficulty we face in explaining or understanding the term unconscious as used in psychoanalysis. Freud himself sums up the matter in a concise, deeply clarifying passage from his last work, *An Outline of Psychoanalysis*:

> In our science as in the others the problem is the same: behind the attributes (qualities) of the object under examination which are presented to our perception, we have to discover something else which approximates more closely to what may be supposed

to be the real state of affairs. We have no hope of being able to reach the latter itself, since it is evident that everything new that we have inferred must nevertheless be translated back into the language of our perceptions, from which it is simply impossible to free ourselves.

This passage leads to the final point I want to make about the difficulty of understanding Darwin and Freud. Although the *problem* is the same in all the sciences our *response* to it is not the same. The cognitive challenge indicated here is, after all, shared also by such respectably hard sciences as physics and astronomy. Even when our perceptual capacities are extended by microscopes and telescopes, the evidence that the hard sciences provide must be supplemented by inferences and theoretical assumptions. Yet we are hardly concerned about the absence, in explanations of physics or astronomy, of a story with a moral drift whereas we demand precisely that from Darwin's biology and Freud's psychology. The reason for this difference is, I think, fairly obvious. These two sciences deal much more closely with questions and issues that define for us what it means to be human. It is not easy for us to think about their findings neutrally because we want from them some moral direction, a narrative that inspires or consoles.

Finally, I want to make clear that reliance on metaphors of agency and purpose does not compromise the truth and value of Darwin's and Freud's theories. But it is important to remember that metaphorical explanations are shortcuts and that shortcuts tend to make disturbing ideas more acceptable. Beyond that acknowledgment, I am not arguing in this essay that these great theories *cannot* be understood. My title, after all, indicates as much, for it alerts us to *the difficulty, not the impossibility*, of understanding Darwin and Freud.

When Novelists Compete with Freud

We are familiar with the problems that arise when literature is examined from a Freudian point of view. But what follows when ambitious novelists are spurred to replace his picture of mind with one of their own, a picture competitive with his? I will discuss this competitive practice in the work of three such writers born in successive generations after Freud's own: D. H. Lawrence, Iris Murdoch and Marilynne Robinson. Their world views might loosely be called religious – loosely because, despite their attraction to formal religions, they are imaginatively independent. Conversely, Freud's theoretical work, despite its scientific character, is akin to imaginative creation, to mythmaking. My aim in clarifying the difference between their art and his science is to better understand the overlapping conceptual ground between them.

We can get to the heart of the matter by contrasting the metaphors of depth used by Lawrence, Murdoch and Robinson with the Freudian metaphor. For Lawrence, the idea of depth is linked to the image of *descent*, for Murdoch with the image of *ascent*, and for Robinson with the image of *extension* – three different imaginings but all of them employed to express *felt experience*. In Freud's so-called depth psychology, the metaphor has a different significance. What is said to be deep or unconscious in psychoanalysis are desires and fears that have undergone motivated forgetting and are therefore said to be *repressed*. A psychoanalyst may question the truth of a patient's report of felt experience, alert to possible evidence of resistance to some repressed material, but what then becomes important is the procedure of teasing out that material, a matter of *inference* rather than direct report. Successful inference – insight – leads to a measure of conviction on the part of patients when it makes a connection with their conscious thinking, typically accompanied by surprise or embarrassment or weakening denial. This aim differs sharply from that of depth-seeking novelists who seek to capture and transmit the resonance of felt experience.

Lawrence's most explicit account of his competition with Freud was set down in two tracts, *Psychoanalysis and the Unconscious* and *Fantasia of the Unconscious*, written in quick succession at the midpoint of his career. We may smile on discovering that a novelist who had acquired notoriety for the sexual content of his work should so aggressively challenge a psychologist who had acquired a similar reputation. Or that the author of *Sons and Lovers*, a book that was admired for its insight into the role of the incest motive in human development, should attack a psychologist who offered insight into the same subject. But neither of these tracts mounts an informed critique of Freud's ideas. (The second one makes no attempt to do so.) Lawrence is plainly seeking not the Freudian unconscious but a more vital kind of *consciousness*.

Lawrence's psychology features two opposing kinds of consciousness, one less vital (and more familiar) than the other. They are, in his work, variously labeled: mental *vs.* blood, spiritual *vs.*

sensual, ideal *vs.* spontaneous, social *vs.* individual, civilized *vs.* pristine. His argument is that internalizing the prevailing biases of civilization prejudices us against authentic sensuality and thus corrupts consciousness. This led him to alter Freud's explanation of the incest motive. A sensual attachment to the mother in his view would not arise if the child is let alone; the trouble stems from the culture's sentimental love-ideal imposed upon the child unknowingly by the mother. This kind of reasoning in Lawrence (and in Rousseau, his chief precursor in this regard) leads him to take a view of the human situation that is pessimistic and optimistic at the same time. On the one hand, the corruptive influence of civilization is pervasive and enchains the mind; on the other, it is the product of an alterable social system of values, not an inevitable complication of human development, and so the possibility of a fundamental change, of "rebirth," is always present. A symbolic death, a descent into the underworld of "dark gods," could, as it were, re-educate our sexual consciousness, sloughing off corruptive civilized influence. One striking instance in his work of tension between these modes of consciousness is the thesis developed in his keen critique, *Studies in Classic American Literature*, in which a literary work's more overt and culturally acceptable intentions are associated with "the artist" while its potent, less acceptable implications are linked with "the tale." Thus the often-quoted tag of this depth-seeking literary critic: Never trust the Artist, trust the Tale.

Near the beginning of *Psychoanalysis and the Unconscious*, Lawrence states an objection to Freud, the aggressiveness of which derives less from disagreement than from frustration. The psychoanalyst, he finds, does not or will not construct a morally informed view of the world: "He can't get down to the rock on which he would build his church." What, in other words, does the man believe? What does he offer as a would-be healer? Freud would have replied that the task of his   psychotherapy was to enable the patient to build or rebuild his or her beliefs, but this answer would not have satisfied his religiously minded critic.

Iris Murdoch praised Freud insofar as she understood that he endorsed an expanded, Platonic conception of sexuality, an Eros that was not narrowly biological but pervasively and profoundly psychological. Her novels, like his theories and therapies, explore the vicissitudes of our erotic entanglements, although she does not examine their infantile origins. Moreover, the prime target of investigation in the two cases is not so different – in the one vanity and other manifestations of egoistic fantasy; in the other, the ego's mechanisms of defense against painful self-revelation. But there is also a major difference between the two projects, and it amounts to an opposition.

The ambition of psychoanalytic therapy, she understood, was melioristic, no more. It sought to make the lives of neurotics less painful, more satisfying. Murdoch sensed correctly that, for Freud, it is not possible for human beings to win more than a measure of freedom from the consequences of their prolonged infantile dependence. *Her* moral vision entailed the hope of more radical change. She sought to cleanse the soul of error, error that was admittedly tenacious but curable because it derived from faulty seeing rather than faulty being. We are in her view like the creatures in Plato's cave who mistake the images seen by firelight for the true forms illuminated by the sun. Accordingly, her novels abundantly dramatize false imitations of the Good even as they honor also the Good as a sovereign ideal that exerts an ever-magnetic influence over our moral consciousness.

What exactly constitutes Murdoch's alternative explanation of illusion or misperception, the nub of her creative competition with Freud? Observing that tragedy in literature is a "comfort word" designed to help us bear suffering rather than transcend it, she wants us to understand that the motives invoked to account for tragic outcomes – obsession, envy, guilt, remorse and the like – derive from our egoism, our vanity. When we look at the human scene truly, from above rather than from below as Freud does, we understand motives in impersonal terms, governed by Chance and Necessity rather than by choice and the constraints on choice, their psychological equivalents. Her novels offer us three kinds of exceptional persons capable of intuiting this wisdom, capable of what she liked to call unselfing, a coinage adapted from Simone Weil's coinage "*décreation.*" One path to unselfing is by way of radical ascesis, a perfected, saintly attention to others rather than self. The other two paths, more transient but equally authentic, are falling in love (Plato would have approved) and artistic creation (Plato would not have approved). In all these cases, self-transcendence is implied, which from a Freudian point of view approximates religious illusion.

The American novelist and essayist Marilynne Robinson (born 1943) is a newer name, but her novels (*Housekeeping*, *Gilead*, *Home* and *Lila*) along with her essays collected in two books, *The Death of Adam: Essays on Modern Thought* and *Absence of Mind: The Dispelling of Inwardness from The Modern Myth of the Self*, have established her reputation as a novelist and essayist with an authentic individual vision.

Creative competition with Freud also marks her work. Her essays attack modern skeptical thinkers with a very broad brush, from Hobbes up through Feuerbach, Darwin, Nietzsche and

Freud. These writers in her view have degraded the human image, picturing man as selfish and guilt-ridden, and are thus responsible for "the death of Adam" – that is, of man created in the image of God. Robinson finds Freud to be the thinker above all others who has contributed to the baleful distrust of everything noble that pervades the modern sensibility. For her, the honorific psychological term is "subjectivity," our means of looking at the world not analytically but holistically as felt experience, which is the experience of openness to the created world, to the nobility of creation. The mind thus understood becomes a place of piety and reverence rather than of complexes and conflicts. The idea of depth in her work is, then, imaged by extension, by reaching out from self to family to society to the God-inspired wholeness of the created world.

But Robinson also obliges us to understand that this subjectively achieved unity is threatened by the possibility of rupture. (We could hardly take her idealism seriously if she did not acknowledge some such difficulty.) The essays focus on threats arising from social injustice, environmental degradation and skeptical philosophy. The novels eloquently focus on threats deriving from familial tension and the consequent difficulty of maintaining the wholeness of lived experience. What she finds most objectionable in Freud is not any important part of his theory or therapy but his hostility to religion, more precisely his tendency to dis-authenticate religious *experience*. Seeking to free us from illusion, he offers nothing "to touch our essential selves." (Feuerbach, odd as it seems, is a hero for her because his romantic humanism, though atheistic, conveys the quality of religious experience while sacrificing religious belief.) Like Lawrence, Robinson can't see what Freud believes or feels, positively.

Where then does she turn for inspiration in her quest for a religious humanism? To our astonishment her moral hero is John Calvin, a name long associated with belief in the *unworthiness* of man. Her use of Calvin, however, is highly original, both aesthetically and psychologically. Robinson manages to discover something profoundly democratic in the Calvinist idea that "everyone is equally unworthy and equally dependent on the free intervention of grace." The fall of man is potentially a source of joy for all. "When the idea of our moral insufficiency to the world" occurs together with the idea of "the world's insufficiency to us, the sacred beauty of Creation becomes dazzlingly apparent." In such critical moments, our minds, inspired by God, bring into being this necessary sufficiency.

Fear and hope are subtly interrelated in Robinson's fictional worlds. Each of her novels dramatizes the strain on those who try to hold a family together, a goal challenged by a disruptive family member who arouses anxiety in the others. But, as the end of *Housekeeping* makes clear, faith may also spring *from* the fear of desolation. "Whatever we may lose," affirms the young narrator, "very craving gives it back to us again." In another wording of the same idea, "memory pulls us *forward*...every sorrow suggests a thousand songs, and every song a thousand sorrows." For her, the profound conviction that dissolution itself contains the promise of restoration is supported by the Bible understood as a whole, a work in which "the first event is known to have been an expulsion and the last is hoped to be a reconciliation and return." The Bible for her, we may add after reading her commanding essay in the Christmas 2012 issue of the *New York Times Book Review*, is truly an all-inclusive book, and with its help she expands her metaphor of depth-by-extension so that it includes in the space it opens up *all* of literature, from Dante and Milton down to the plainest of realistic novels.

Robinson's just published novel *Lila* tells the story of a young woman, severely neglected by parents and brought up by a drifter and her band of companions, who, despite loneliness and poverty, manages to develop some toughness and even sympathy for the suffering of others. Although her essays inveigh against the social ills dramatized here, Robinson told a reader that Lila's loneliness is not be seen as a problem but as a condition, in line with the Calvinist teaching, cited by her character Reverend Ames, that "people have to suffer to really recognize grace when it comes."

The narrative, set in a small town in Iowa (the book is dedicated "to IoWA"), is shaped by the complex relationship that develops between Lila and Ames whose back story is familiar to us from the earlier novels. They marry but their relationship remains awkward, complicated by mutual mistrust and fear, but it is meant to suggest this "grace," symbolized by the baptism Ames extends to her and by her pregnancy with its promise of continuity – a temporal extension of the metaphor of depth, supplementing the spatial use of it so eloquent in *Housekeeping*. The focus shifts in the latter half of the novel to the heroine's consciousness, a place where painful and often sordid memories threaten to overwhelm a husband's Calvinist instruction and overt concern for the future of his wife and child after his death. A knife that Lila carries and often recalls, implying separation and death, is in symbolic competition with the image of baptism, a ceremony she recently underwent and looks forward to for her child. Robinson will not assure us that continuity represents the more likely outcome, but this novel, like her others, effectively dramatizes *religious experience*, the appreciation of which she found to be lacking in the writings of Freud.

An early draft of this paper, in which I characterized Lawrence, Murdoch and Robinson as religious writers and Freud as a scientific one, was leading me to the ridiculously tame conclusion that the two parties should try to be nicer to one another. I then came to realize that it was not quite correct to describe the three novelists as religious. They are attracted to religious ideas, but they are too individualistic to be spokespersons for any institutional religion. They are not interested in doctrine as such, indifferent to the politics of moral regulation, and, above all, committed to their beliefs on an altogether individual basis, as in each case a party of one. Because their art is conceptually ambitious, they might best be described as literary mythmakers, and their blending of fiction and non-fiction might best be described as mythmaking.

That shift of terminology led me to another, more interesting realization. I came to see that there are really two Freuds in the picture, not always easy to separate. One contributes to a literature of knowledge, the other to a literature of power, to employ a distinction introduced by Thomas De Quincey. Freud the first is a scientific investigator, addressing himself to particular problems, theoretical and practical, and devising a particular therapeutic technique. This is work that is used and improved upon by others. Freud the second is a moral philosopher in spite of himself, whose distinctive achievement was to create a grand narrative of individual psychological development. Like Darwin's comprehensive narrative of human evolution, it altered a whole culture's way of understanding itself. It became in the words of the poet W. H. Auden, "a climate of opinion."

I think it is fair to describe the work of this second Freud as a kind of mythmaking, remembering what he wrote in his famous Letter to Einstein published under the title of "Why War": "does not every science come in the end to a kind of mythology?" Formally speaking, we may connect his theories not only with Darwin's but also with the fictions of such major literary mythmakers as Dante, Milton, Goethe and Beckett. And I think we may also draw into this parallel the work of our three novelist-essayists, which is different from Freud's in its kind and degree of influence but similar to his in the scope and purpose of its imaginative reach.

Memory in Proust and Cognitive Neuroscience, with a Coda on the Mind-Brain Problem

Because memory is a crucial idea both in Marcel Proust's great novel and in contemporary cognitive neuroscience, a comparison of the two cases may tell us something about the modern connection between art and science. I will group Proust's insights under four headings that have scientific standing – Involuntary Memory, Inaccurate Memory, Memory and Self, Memory and Time – and, on that basis, take a fresh look at the challenging mind-brain problem.

The strategies of artistic and scientific work are, of course, different: the artist values originality of expression and multiple implications whereas the scientist seeks repeatable results based on data strictly defined. But this general difference is partly offset in this particular case by the fact that Proust's novel is animated by a sort of scientific passion, including generalized pronouncements and what it likes to call "*les lois psychologiques.*" At one point it explicitly compares the artist's use of impression to the scientist's use of experimentation, and at another it aligns the use of metaphor in literature with the concept of causality in science. This of course is not to say, foolishly, that Proust Was a Neuroscientist, only that he was an early example on the literary side of the spirit of rapprochement between art and science that has developed more noticeably over the last half-century.

As if in response to C. P. Snow's lament in the 1950s concerning their mutual disregard, many novelists and dramatists in the years since have embraced scientific literacy, and, correspondingly, many neuroscientists now reach across the old divide. In fact, a prominent and pervasive idea today, fostered by neuroscientists, is that our genetic inheritance is plastic and modified throughout our lifetime by environmental and cultural influence.[1] Along with the inevitable talk of neurons, synapses, axons, dendrites and so forth, they often directly address the difficult (and, for humanists, cardinal) question of consciousness: how to get from brain to mind, how "to get over the hump from electrochemistry to feeling."[2] The question is fascinating but complicated by the fact that mind, unlike brain, cannot be perceived so that any description of it must be metaphorical. Freud knew that, calling his picture of mind a "metapsychology," and the contemporary neuroscientist Mark Solms reminds us that, since our direct knowledge is limited by our senses, our picture of mind will always be a figurative one."[3] That is indeed the reason why my

---

[1] Here is a brief sample: "The plasticity of the nervous system – the ability of nerve cells to change the strength and even the number of synapses – is the mechanism underlying learning and long-term memory" (Kandel 218); "As neural currents develop, variant individual experiences leave imprints such that no two brains are identical, even those of identical twins" (Edelman, *Second Nature*, 21); "While the basic plan of the brain's organization is... predetermined by our genes....the overall plan is dramatically modified by *environmental influences* during life" (Solms and Turnbull 10-11); "Genes are enablers, not constrainers" (Ridley 250).

[2] John Searle, quoted in Solms and Turnbull, 47, 50.

[3] Solms and Turnbull, 57, 291.

comments on the mind-brain problem will have to focus on two concepts dealing with *brain* functioning – matter and causation.

Involuntary Memory

Proust's novel features the idea that certain past memories, after a period of forgetting, can be recaptured if cued by an association in present time. Such forgetting is not the result of repression in the Freudian sense, where a specific counterforce is involved, but is inevitable because the so-called self is really "a succession of selves." Our ever-changing emotional state is nicely described by the narrator as "the intermittence of the heart." In developing his conception of involuntary memory, Proust was doubtless influenced by Montaigne's idea of mind as fluid and shifting and by Bergson's emphasis on spontaneous memory activated by a present perception that enables *re-cognition*.[4]

Neuroscience helps to explain both the persistence and the power of involuntary memories. Long-term memories are consolidated through repeated modification. They are formed in the hippocampus, which is always supplied with new neurons, and strengthened in the cortical regions where neurons continue to form new terminals. Repetition, however, both in neuroscience and in Proust, is an ambiguous advantage. Eric Kandel distinguishes between merely habitual stimuli, which an animal learns to ignore, and gradually conditioned stimuli, which strengthen

---

4 Bergson, *Matter and Memory*, 95, 105. However, Bergson is always the philosopher, intent on the conceptual relation of mind to matter and thus he ignores emotional factors (involved, for example, in mis-remembering) to which the artist is always sensitive.

memory.⁵ Proust's novel makes a similar distinction between "*l'Habitude*, a repetition that protectively dulls our responses to fresh experience, and another kind of recurrent experience that dissolves habit and enhances life. In such remembering we are always reworking the original experience. In other words, the charm and power of such involuntary memories has much to do with the fact that they gather associations over time and depend on the emotion inherent in the present moment that triggers their releases.⁶ The critic Roger Shattuck comments acutely that the narrator does not record original experience of his privileged moments as major events: "He barely registered any taste or odor of the tea-soaked *madeleine* when Aunt Léonie offered him a piece."⁷ Similarly the past moment when Marcel's grandmother bent down to lace his boots is scarcely noted whereas the experience of remembering it after her death, triggered by his own bending down, releases an eloquent meditation.⁸

The richness of these privileged moments, then, has mainly to do with the narrator's ability in present time to make creative use of involuntary memory. The neuroscientist Daniel Schacter, devoting some pages to Proust in his book *Searching for Memory*, observes that involuntary memories in the narrative "gradually

---

5   Kandel 160-61.

6   A Proust chronologist has figured out that the Combray experiences took place in the early 1890s whereas the day when "le narrateur prend une tasse de thé et une petite madeleine" took place in 1919-20. See CHRNOLOGIE DES PRINCIPAUX ÉVÉNEMENTS D'À LA RECHERCHE DU TEMPS PERDU selon Willy Haches." *Bulletin de la Société des Amis de Marcel Proust et des Amis de Combray* (No. 6, 1956).

7   Shattuck, Marcel Proust, 120, 123.

8   Samuel Beckett commented about this meditation that Proust "never wrote better." Beckett, *Proust*, 25.

become more voluntary."[9] Indeed, we may add, they positively cluster toward the end as the narrator begins to merge with the author and to articulate a guiding aesthetic.[10]

Inaccurate Memory

If the self is really a succession of selves, it follows that an individual's memories will be inconsistent with one another and even inaccurate fundamentally because there remains no reliable base memory by which the original truth behind these modifications may be judged. We are accustomed to connect our very identity with the reliability of memory, but Proust's narrator asserts, and the novel demonstrates, that "a memory which we believed to be old and authentic has been refashioned by us many times." Freud, back in 1899, came to a similar conclusion regard-

---

9   Schacter, 25-6.

10 It is worth noting further that the most memorable of the privileged moments involves the interlocking senses of taste and smell. The novel itself comments that smell is both the most fragile and most enduring of our senses, and neuroscience bears this out. In evolutionary terms smell/taste is the most primitive sense and the one most closely associated with the amygdala, hence with emotions before they have been worked over by intellect. (In this connection see Joseph LeDoux, "The Mysterious Underpinnings of Emotional Life.") It is also true, as Jonah Lehrer notes (68), that the "olfactory bulb is inundated with feedback from higher bran regions: so that intellect may well feel overpowered by olfactory sensations." Rudyard Kipling intuited this in a line of verse: "Smells are surer than sights or sounds to make your heartstrings crack" ("Lichtenberg" in *The Five Nations*). When the more sophisticated senses of sight and sound are appealed to in Proust's narrative, we notice that an almost essayistic style replaces a mainly dramatic one. The sight of the Martinville spires from a moving coach inspires Marcel to compose a descriptive account that he deliberately imports into the text. And the "little phrase" from Vinteuil's sonata that enchants Swann must be heard more than once and even studied before its charm becomes fixed in his mind.

ing memories of childhood, which, he wrote, were largely reconstructions or "screen memories," though therapeutically useful because they reflected real if not original emotions. Contemporary cognitive neuroscience has broadened the point, judging reconstruction to be the general rule regarding memory retrieval. Schacter has summed up neatly current thinking on this topic: "it is a long-standing myth that memories are passive or literal recordings of reality....A feeling of memory depends as much on what is happening in the present as on what happened in the past.... For better or worse our memories are largely at the mercy of our elaborations."[11]

The novelist seized on this insight, making errors of memory and illusions of identity the very material of his narrative. He explained to an editor: "I am obliged to depict errors without feeling obliged to say that I consider them to be errors. Too bad for me if the reader believes that I consider them the truth."[12] Proust's psychological interest at such moments is closer in spirit to phenomenology than psychoanalysis, but self-deception is an important subject for both Proust and Freud. What the neuroscientist might want to add is the idea that a thought begins as a bodily stimulus and physiological response (it is in that special sense "unconscious") and then becomes conscious so that feeling it precedes thinking it.

---

[11] Schacter, 5, 25, 56. Edelman makes the point more technically: "[Memory] is recategorical: it does not replicate an original experience exactly....Nonlinear interactions in a multidimensional network of neuronal groups...allow a non-identical 'reliving' of a set of prior acts and events, yet there is often the illusion that one is recalling an event exactly as it happened." (*Wider Than the Sky*, 52.)

[12] Kolb, ed. *Marcel Proust et Jacques Rivière: Correspondance*, p. 3.

Memory and Self

In Kandel's words, "Memory is essential not only for the continuity of individual identity but also for the transmission of culture and for the evolution and continuity of societies over centuries."[13] Neuroscientists call this continuity, when applied to individuals, an "autobiographical self," denoting the ability of human beings to describe their personal history from about the age of seven as a coherent sequence of episodes. The writer of so elaborately quasi-autobiographical a work as *A la Recherche du temps perdu* did not of course lack this ability, but his narrator highlights the theme of fragmentary identity from the very first sentence: *Longtemps je me suis couché de bonne heure*. The boundaries of *Longtemps* are undefined; self is divided between a subject *je* and an object *me*; and the verb tense, the so-called *passé composé*, is neither simply past nor present but a combination, unusual in the subsequent narrative, of a present auxiliary and a past participle.[14] Moreover, Marcel is in bed slipping back and forth between sleep and waking. And he confuses his own identity with that of characters in the book he's been reading. No doubt this opening is artful, as are many later passages concerning the fluidity and dispersion of individual identity. In fact the struggle to achieve enough psychic integration to write an ambitious work of art is an overarching theme of the novel, and we understand toward the end that the work in question will resemble the one we have been reading. It will be a novel in which the very gaps and incon-

---

13 Kandel, 10.

14 Concerning the grammar of the novel's first sentence I am indebted to Shattuck, *Proust's Binoculars*, 80-81.

sistencies of memory and self compose themselves into a vast and complex whole.

Neuroscientists too understand the importance for psychic functioning of a coherent sense of selfhood based on autobiographical memory. Schacter writes: "in order to be experienced as memory, the retrieved information must be collected in the context of a particular time and place and with some reference to oneself as a participant in the episode."[15] This implies that human memory, unlike a computer's, does not just retrieve isolated bits of information but gathers associations in relation to an organizing self. In its logical prowess the brain resembles a computer, but its operations are not algorithmic. Much of human understanding is based not on logic but on pattern recognition, involving the interaction of the brain's systems and circuits. Evolution has even included redundancy or what neuroscientists call "degeneracy," a word referring to "the ability of structurally different elements of a system to perform the same function or yield the same output."[16] Natural selection, according to Edelman, has sacrificed specificity and precision for the sake of richness of metaphorical reach.

Memory and Time

The narrator finally understands that the way the present is inhabited by the past demonstrates the mind's power to transcend experienced time, the power to live not only in the present but also in a past time that must and can be imagined. Not that

---

15 Schacter, 17.
16 Edelman, *Wider Than the Sky*, 43; also *Second Nature*, 33.

time's destructive action is ever denied. The old charm of Gilberte and Odette in the Champs Elysées is gone forever; the Dreyfus affair and the War have ripped to pieces the old social fabric; old friends have died or decayed into unseemly old age; and the present Princesse de Guermantes, a name that so enchanted young Marcel, is none other than Mme. de Verdurin, known to us earlier as a bourgeois snob and social climber. But time can be regained when the immediately experienced present and the imagined past are coordinated. Shattuck describes Proust's vision as both "binocular" and "stereoscopic," meaning that past and present are seen as both divided and joined.[17] The narrator calls his final joined vision "extra-temporal" but not because he wants to teach the idolatry of art. Rather he believed that a book's ultimate value lay in its ability to let readers read themselves. By "extra-temporal" he meant the ability of human beings to experience and imagine at one and the same time, enabling them, for all their physical limitations, to live in what he called the third dimension, the vast dimension of Time.

Proust's conception of memory and time is illuminated by distinguishing what we share and don't share with animals. Dogs and cats have brains very similar to ours (which, alas, makes them useful for laboratory purposes). They can remember, they can solve problems, up to a point they can communicate. In some sense, then, they can think. But the much greater development of the cortical regions in human brains enables us to do something other animals cannot do: think about thinking. As Edelman explains, only humans can conceptualize a past and future time,

---

17 Shattuck, *Proust's Binoculars*, 42-51, in particular this sentence on page 51: "the stereoscopic principle allows the binocular vision of mind to hold contradictory aspects of things in a steady perspective of recognition."

and only humans can relate a sequence of temporal moments to a nameable self.[18] The only time we actually experience is what Edelman calls "the remembered present." Although we may suppose that we experience the whole flow of time from the past into the future, this is an illusion. For human beings with higher-order consciousness, the past and future are conceptual constructs."[19] This helps us see that a Proustian phrase like "freed from the order of time" is not a literary idealization. The unique human ability to think about thinking does liberate us from the constraint of experienced time.

Coda

Encouraged by these linkages, let us take a fresh look at the stubborn mind-brain problem, particularly at what those interested in explaining consciousness call the "hard problem," how one bridges the gap between the activity of neurons and human emotions. Even the so-called "easy" problem – to find specific neural correlates for the emotions – is not really easy once we learn that nerve cells act not in isolation but as interacting populations or systems. But the challenge of the hard problem is irresistible because it confronts us with the stubborn difficulty of discarding the old Cartesian dualism of mind and matter. Solms and Turnbull, for example, write, "we are made of only one type of stuff." Doubtless they know that stuff (*der Stoff*) is the regular German word for physical matter. It looks as if they are robustly embracing materialism, but they must add, "this stuff is per-

---

18 Edelman, *Second Nature*, 15.
19 Edelman, *Wider than the Sky*, 134.

ceived in two different ways." While apparently discarding dualism, they introduce it again by way of their ambiguous locution "dual-aspect monism."[20]

This maneuver is hard to avoid, and illustrates how tough our problem is. But I think we can at least make a dent in it if we change the word matter to *process*. Over a century ago, William James conceived of consciousness as process, and the idea has been seized on and amplified by Edelman, who writes: "in modern science, matter [also] has been reconceived in terms of processes [whereas] mind has not been reconceived as a special form of matter."[21]

The second seemingly inevitable word that has complicated our thinking about the hard problem is "causation." And here again Edelman's Darwinian orientation to neuroscience provides clarification. Long ago our ancestors came down from the trees and began to walk on two legs. That made possible the expansion of the brain's cortical regions and eventually the modification of the larynx for speech, leading to the creation of a language capable, as no other animal's language is capable, of syntax and symbolism. The many changes that we have undergone in our evolutionary development have been so random and complex that, though they have been made possible by natural selection, it seems imprecise to say they have been *caused* by it. When we consider human behavior we need not rule out the concept of cause but we need to recognize that, in the words of Matt Ridley,

---

20 Solms and Turnbull, 56.
21 Edelman, *Bright Air, Brilliant Fire, On the Matter of Mind*, 6-7. James's brilliant anticipatory insight is found chiefly in the essay "Does Consciousness Exist?" See *William James: The Essential Writings*. Edited by Bruce W. Wilshire, 162-67.

"The cause of behavior lies in a circular, not a linear, system."[22] We tend to think of cause and effect as a linear phenomenon, but when so much neural circularity is involved, this is a weak way of explaining human behavior. It would be better to say with Edelman: "the very complexity of the brain's repertoires [means that] every act of perception is to some degree an act of creation, and every act of memory is to some degree an act of imagination."[23]

In sum, if we take account of this high degree of complexity and circular interaction, we find that there can be no direct answer to the question of how we get from neuronal activity to consciousness, hence whether any cause-and-effect analysis can help much to explain the relation of brain to mind. About the most we can say is that the brain *entails* consciousness and makes it possible. And with that I must leave it.

Works Cited

Beckett, Samuel. *Proust.* New York: Grove Press, [1931] 1957.

Bergson, Henri. *Matter and Memory.* Translated by Nancy Margaret Paul and W. Scott Palmer. London: Allen & Unwin, 1962.

Damasio, Antonio M. *Descartes' Error: Emotion, Reason, and the Human Brain.* New York: Penguin, 1994.

———. *The Feeling of What Happens: Body and Emotion in the Making of Consciousness.* Harcourt Brace: New York, San Diego, London, 1999.

---

[22] Matt Ridley, *The Agile Gene*, 273.
[23] Edelman, *Second Nature*, 100.

Edelman, Gerald M. *Bright Air, Brilliant Fire: On the Matter of Mind*, New York: Basic Books, 1992.

____. *The Remembered Present: A Biological Theory of Consciousness*. New York: Basic Books, 1989.

____. *Second Nature: brain science and human knowledge.* New Haven: Yale UP.

____. *Wider than the Sky: The Phenomenal Gift of Consciousness.* New Haven: Yale UP, 2004.

Freud, Sigmund. "Screen Memories." *Standard Edition of the Psychological Works.* Vol. III, 303-322.

____. "The Unconscious." *Standard Edition of the Psychological Works.* Vol. XIV, 166-215.

James, William. "Does Consciousness Exist?" *William James: The Essential Writings.* Albany: State University of New York, 1984.

Kolb, Philip, ed. *Marcel Proust et Jacques Rivière: Correspondance (1914-1922).* Paris: Plon, 1955.

Haches, Willy. CHRONOLOGIE DES PRINCIPAUX ÉVÈNEMENTS D'A LA RECHERCHE DU TEMPS PERDU. *Bulletin de la Société des Amis de Marcel Proust et des Amis de Combray* (No. 6. 1956).

Kandel, Eric R. *In Search of Memory: The Emergence of a New Science of Mind.* New York: W.W. Norton Inc., 2006.

Kipling, Rudyard. *The Five Nations.* New York: Doubleday, 1903.

LeDoux, Joseph E. *The Emotional Brain: the mysterious underpinnings of emotional life.* New York: Simon and Shuster, 1996.

Lehrer, Jonah. *Proust Was a Neuroscientist.* Houghton Mifflin: Boston and New York, 2007.

Proust, Marcel. *Remembrance of Things Past* and *In Search of Lost Time.* Translated by C. K. Scott-Moncrieff, Terence Kilmartin, D. J. Enright, Andreas Mayor, 1956-2003.

Ridley, Matt. *The Agile Gene: how nature turns on nurture.* New York: Harper Collins. 2003.

Schacter, Daniel L. *Searching for Memory: the Brain, the Mind, and the Past*. New York: Basic Books, 1996.

Shattuck, Roger. *Marcel Proust*. Princeton: Princeton UP, 1979, 1982.

_____. *Proust's Binoculars: a study of memory, time and imagination in "A la Recherche du temps perdu"*. New York: Random House, 1963.

Solms, Mark & Oliver Turnbull. *The Brain and the Inner World: an introduction to the neuroscience of subjective experience*. New York: Other Press, 2002.

Imagining One's Own Death: Freud and the Poets

In his great essay of 1915, "Thoughts for the Times on War and Death," Freud comments: "It is indeed impossible to imagine our own death; and whenever we make the attempt to do so we can perceive that we are in fact still present as spectators."[24] Taking for granted our perception that we will die, Freud focuses on the problem of *imagining* our own non-existence. This may seem a merely logical problem stemming from the fact that we tend to equate being able to imagine non-existence with being able to know or perceive it directly.[25] But the psychological problem of imagining is different. Influenced by its unconscious component, our imagining self cannot tolerate the idea of non-existence. As Freud put it, "in the unconscious we are convinced of our own immortality." He could have fortified this statement by adding that

---

24 Freud, *Standard Edition; of the Psychological Works*, XIV, 289.
25 An article by Jesse Bering in *Scientific American* (October 22, 2008) titled "Never Say Die: Why We Can't Imagine Death" seems to focus as Freud does on a psychological problem but really presents it as a logical one, as when Bering cites with approval a philosopher who writes: "When I try to imagine my own non-existence I have to imagine that I perceive or know about my non-existence." This equating of imagining with conscious perceiving leads Bering and his philosopher to miss Freud's insight.

we never dream our own death, though we often enough dream the death of others. Or, to put it more carefully, on those very rare occasions when we are *about* to dream our own death, we wake up screaming and call our dream a nightmare.

How, then, have poets met this challenging problem, for good poets, almost by definition, extend the limits of what can be imagined? Before the eighteenth-century Enlightenment, religion lent its support for belief in an afterlife, and so the need to replace belief with an inward turn of some kind, with the account of some psychological action, was hardly apparent. But the challenge to do so could not be evaded thereafter. And this paper will attempt to show how some post- Enlightenment poets, in the West, have managed it.

The post-Enlightenment poet shifts the reader's attention from afterlife mythology to the means by which the mind expresses the experience of *anticipating* its own annihilation. We can, I think, distinguish three broad phases of this shift of poetic attention. The first is coeval with the Romantic period and comes across vividly in poems by Lord Byron and Giacomo Leopardi. Both recoiled from the idea that life, stripped of illusions, amounted to nothingness, and led to a sense of futility. But they stressed also man's heroic resistance to this knowledge. They imagined Death (a word the Romantics typically capitalized) as a kind of presence, and their opposition to it drew energy from their very desperation.

A second phase emerged later in the nineteenth-century, as the agnostic spirit of the age widened and changed the vocabulary of spiritual need. It is well illustrated by Emily Dickinson, who often dramatized the approach of death as a moment of experience that is at once appalling and fascinating. While still rather theatrical, her stance is more personal and private than that of Byron and Leopardi, and she does not so much ignore or scorn Christian doctrine as subject it to her central concern, the drama of consciousness *in extremis*. In one famous poem, "Because I could not stop for Death," the words immortality and eternity only *seem* to allude to an afterlife. They function in the poem to heighten the awesomeness, the inconceivability, of a blanked out world and mind, a void. The last stanza reads: "Since then – 'tis Centuries – and yet/ Feels shorter than the Day/ I first surmised the Horses' Heads/ Were toward Eternity." We are zoomed beyond death only to be zoomed back again to a moment of shocked recognition on the verge of death, captured in a paradox: whole centuries are shorter than the single day on which this was experienced.

    A third phase, I believe, develops near the middle of the twentieth-century, and may be illustrated by the later poetry of Wallace Stevens. Stevens absorbed from a Zeitgeist influenced by thinkers like Freud and Wittgenstein the idea that, since death is not an event in life, not experienced, we can know nothing about it.

    In contrast to Dickinson, he turns away from explicit address to the subject and dramatizes instead, and with subtle vigor, the process of decline. The quieter, less theatrical tone of poems belonging to this phase should be understood as a new acceptance of the fact that the fear of death cannot be expunged; hence the modes of direct confrontation in favor earlier are no longer imaginatively rewarding.[26] Poetry of this phase is more openly aware

---

26 Philip Larkin writes to this point in his famous poem, "Aubade," in which he scorns the idea of arguing against this fear of death:"Specious stuff that says: *No rational being / Can fear a thing it will not feel, not seeing* / That this is what we fear – no sight, no sound, / No touch or taste or smell, nothing to think with / Nothing to love or link with / The anesthetic from which none come round."

of its own metaphors and procedures. It shows us that the mind holds its own against the void more by way of style than statement. Modern poetry, Seamus Heaney believes, offers instead of defiance the subtler consolation of "redress, setting its fine excess in the balance against all of life's inadequacies, desolations, and atrocities."[27]

We may lend more concreteness to these general remarks by examining closely two particular poems, "I heard a Fly buzz when I died" by Emily Dickinson and "Of Mere Being" by Wallace Stevens.

Here is the first of these:

> I heard a Fly buzz – when I died –
> The Stillness in the Room
> Was like the Stillness in the Air –
> Between the heaves of Storm –
>
> The Eyes around – had wrung them dry –
> And Breaths were gathering firm
> For that last Onset – when the King
> Be witnessed – in the Room –
>
> I willed my Keepsakes – Signed away
> What portions of me be
> Assignable – and then it was
> There interposed a Fly –
>
> With Blue – uncertain stumbling Buzz –
> Between the light – and me –

---

[27] Seamus Heaney, *The Redress of Poetry* (1995), p. 163.

> And then the Windows failed — and then
> I could not see to see.

The speaker necessarily reports the moment of death retrospectively but concentrates our attention on that moment. All preparation for death, like the willing of keepsakes, has been completed, and the only thing the dying person attends to is the sound of stillness and buzz — a stillness big with expectation. It is a moment when "the King be witnessed in the Room." The word "King" is a canny choice, engaging a secular perspective without negating a religious one, for it alludes both to the phrase King of Terrors and the phrase Christ the King. But this grand thought is interrupted by the buzz of an insignificant fly that draws our attention down to the psychology of perception, which governs the final stanza. There, three canceling actions occurring in the quickest possible succession define the acutely experienced moment at which consciousness ceases. First, "The Windows failed," a mental failure in the guise of a material one. Then the simultaneous extinction of both, captured in the witty phrase, "I could not see to see." Dickinson jams together the ideas of mental and physical cessation, scorning coolly rational distinctions. She is interested only in the drama of consciousness, kindled here by the appalling and therefore fascinating idea of nothingness.

Here now is Stevens' poem "Of Mere Being," a contrasting imagining of one's own death written in the mid-twentieth century:

> The palm at the end of the mind,
> Beyond the last thought, rises
> In the bronze décor.

> A gold-feathered bird
> Sings in the palm without human hearing,
> Without human feeling, a foreign song.
>
> You know then that it is not the reason
> That makes us happy or unhappy.
> The bird sings. Its feather shine.
>
> The palm stands on the edge of space.
> The wind moves slowly in the branches.
> The bird's fire-fangled feathers dangle down.

The poet is seeking the mereness of being, an approach to the end of meaning this side of death. The interplay of mind and world that had been Stevens' central concern is hardly active anymore. Palm and gold-feathered bird are at the "end" of the mind, "Beyond" the last thought. The imagery itself reminds the reader less of the physical world than of Stevens' exuberant earlier poems. The speaker can of course recall these images but cannot summon any longer the emotion that was once attached to them, and so is obliged to realize and it is not images themselves that make us happy or unhappy. The poem's style of severe simplicity carries the meaning, a quiet descent on unextended wings. Gold coloring, palm, bird, and fire are images associated with desire in its more youthful manifestations, but this poem is seeking the end of desire. The bird sings, the palm stands, the wind moves. And the last line captures one last gaudy flourish, "fire-fangled feathers," before checking it by another alliteration suggestive of sexual finality, "dangles down." It contains no hint of transcendence, protest or even acquiescence. Yet it moves us by placing the human up against the inhuman, by leaning against the void rather than by actively opposing it.

A Dickinson poem seeks to render the sudden consciousness of the moment of death, but the last word for Stevens is a subtle affirmation of the mind's creative process itself. In both cases, however, and this is the point I want to stress, the post-Enlightenment poet's imagining of death involves not only a recognition of death as void but also offers as consolation a tacit tribute to the resourcefulness of the still creative mind. The critic Frank Kermode had in mind this new kind of redress when he commented on Julian Barnes's book about death, *Nothing to Be Frightened Of*: "It seems that nothing really helps any more. We know nothing about the matter [of death] that entitles us to have an opinion of it. But consolations and rewards are to be sought, if anywhere, in appropriately developed fictions... like Barnes's."[28]

At the end of *The Future of an Illusion*, in one of his rare philosophic passages, Freud defends psychology as a genuine science, arguing against those who think that, because its subject is the mind itself, the agent of thought, it cannot attain to the objectivity required of a science. "Our mind," he argues with a nod to Darwin, "has been developed precisely in the attempt to explore the external world and it must therefore have realized in its structure some degree of expediency." Then he adds, "the problem of the nature of the world without regard to our percipient mental apparatus is an empty abstraction, devoid of practical interest."[29] Putting aside the vexed question of psychoanalysis as a science, I find this reasoning forceful in connection with post-Enlightenment poetry that affirms the mind's own strength even as it con-

---

28 *New York Review of Books*, Oct. 9, 2008, p. 40.
29 Freud, *Standard Edition of the Psychological Works*, XXI, 56.

templates the extinction of consciousness. It suggests that all we have access to — this is our limitation and our pride — is our imagining mind, what in Dickinson is represented by the faculties of sight and understanding on the verge of extinction, what Stevens called "the palm at the end of the mind." To think that we can know death apart from such mediation is mere illusion. Such words as we may use in the attempt to do so are "empty abstraction."

Reformulating Freud's Hamlet

Early and late in his psychoanalytic career, Freud promoted his interpretation of Shakespeare's *Hamlet*, which supported his belief that an Oedipus Complex was central to our understanding of human development. The interpretation has not worn well. It consists essentially of two propositions: first, Hamlet is beset by unconscious conflict, oedipal in nature; second, Hamlet is a flawed hero who cannot act as he ought because the task he faces arouses this conflict and cripples his will. So stated, neither of these propositions can be defended today, but, reformulated, they can lead us to a fresh and persuasive reading of Shakespeare's famous and exceedingly complex play.

Hamlet clearly dramatizes a young man's inner conflict, and does so with extraordinary brio and intensity. It is apparent also that this conflict centers on the hero's prolonged inability, for psychological rather than practical reasons, to carry out an act of revenge that he strongly believes he ought to accomplish. Because his inability derives from some inner resistance and because Hamlet himself admits to being baffled by it ("I do not know/ Why yet I live to say 'This thing's to do,'/ Sith [Since] I have cause, and will, and strength, and means,/ To do 't"), it makes sense, or *seems* to make sense, to describe his conflict as *uncon-*

scious. But that word "unconscious" is tricky and requires some parsing.

When we refer to a literary character's unconscious mind, we mean that the character is presented as a person whose language and behavior convey the impression of someone unable (rather than simply unwilling) to acknowledge desires that offend his moral sense but that we, as spectators or readers, are allowed to surmise. Nowadays we think of unconscious conflict in terms of individual psychology, but Hamlet's conflict, I will argue, is presented primarily as expressing a cultural conflict expressed for dramatic effect through an individual. It is therefore clarifying to describe this conflict not as *repressed* (that is, "unconscious" in the psychoanalytic sense) but *recessed*, backgrounded in the play. It is conveyed to an audience by way of the drama's network of implication, over the head, so to speak, of the character who embodies it.

Can we describe this conflict as "oedipal" in the psychoanalytic sense of the word? Nothing in the play allows us to refer Hamlet's problem to psychosexual conflicts experienced in early childhood. But, although the phrase "oedipal conflict" looks anachronistic in discussing a Renaissance play, we can't help noticing that Hamlet often expresses, and in highly charged language, hostility toward his would-be father and, in almost the same breath, sexually charged disgust for his unfaithful mother as well as for his beloved Ophelia. Shakespeare had not heard of an Oedipus Complex, to be sure, but this play (among others by Shakespeare) suggests that he had observed ambitious young men who exhibit strongly conflicted feelings toward figures of authority and toward the women who belong to them. It would not be extravagant to credit him with dramatizing a pre-Freudian insight. But it is important to notice that the pressure of what to some extent resembles what we would call an oedipal conflict cannot be singled out as *the* cause of Hamlet's distress. It is one of many causes.

Shakespeare has taken pains to show that the pressures on Hamlet arise not from past trauma but from the severity of the shock he is currently sustaining as a result of being suddenly uprooted from a world of enchanted innocence and thrust into a world totally different. A picture of those innocent years is created by many clues: his love-letter to Ophelia read by Polonius, his childlike delight and excitement over the reappearance of the Players whom he earlier knew and whose unsophisticated rhetoric rouses his nostalgia, his initial hearty welcome to Rosencrantz and Guildenstern who remind him of his carefree time at Wittenberg, and his tender recollection, in the Gravedigger's scene, of Yorick, his father's court jester, who evidently loved the boy and was loved by him ("He hath borne me on his back a thousand times… Here hung those lips that I have kissed I know not how oft"). That earlier time is now present only in the form of the stern, possibly deceptive ghost of his father, who talks of murder, duty and obligation but not of love, joy or tenderness. Harshly different from that past world is the all too immediate Danish court ruled by Claudius, a corrupt and swinish place of dark secrets, carousing, scheming calculation and of such pervasive hypocrisy that no one in its orbit can afford to take Polonius's good advice about being true to oneself. Most disturbingly, Hamlet suspects (and the Ghost supports his suspicion) that the new king, who now glibly demands to be considered his new father, has murdered his true father. Pressuring Hamlet still more, Shakespeare has isolated him. In the sources of the play Hamlet had the support of both Ophelia and his mother, but both are now creatures of the court, their support nullified.

The dramatized crux of the Prince's conflict, highlighted by the soliloquies, is of course his struggle to overcome his resistance to avenge the murder of King Hamlet by killing King Claudius, an act that he feels both obliged and unable to carry out. What explanation for Hamlet's notorious resistance can replace Freud's, one that has both psychological depth and textual support? I suggest that such an explanation will emerge if we keep in mind two factors: what killing a king means for a Shakespearean protagonist; and what the Ghost truly represents in this play. This explanation proves to be broader than Hamlet is allowed to understand clearly but we sense the pressure it exerts on him. When we consider these causes, we will understand Shakespeare's hero as a man situated in a profoundly conflicted *cultural* moment whose inability to kill the king is not well explained by the idea of neurotic weakness or some such defect of character.

Hamlet regularly refers to Claudius not by name but as "the king," and a reader of Shakespeare's plays hardly needs to be reminded that, in them, an awesome taboo accompanies the act of regicide. Killing a king is tantamount in Shakespeare's world to threatening an entire social order, the very principle of authority that holds a society together. Hamlet hates Claudius but is deeply ambivalent about the act of killing him. It is an act that he cannot disentangle from the thought of his own death and from the sense of death haunting human existence itself, as will become starkly apparent when we look carefully at his "To be or not to be" soliloquy.

His ambivalence regarding the ghost of his father is a more subtle matter because Hamlet emphatically admires his father and reveres his memory. But we can see that the stern Ghost who insists on revenge in terms of honor and obligation and who appears in the first scene of the play in heavy armor decades out of date, represents an older ethical code of blood revenge. Hamlet does not *directly* question this code. But Shakespeare allows us to detect his indirect questioning from the way he represents its exemplification in the two characters who, along with the Ghost, most openly subscribe to it, Laertes and Fortinbras. They are too simply seen by critics as mere foils for Hamlet, their boldness exposing his weakness. But Laertes' idea of honorable revenge is evidently crude: he lets Claudius know he is so eager for it that he "would cut [Hamlet's] throat in a church." The case of Fortinbras is more complicated but more important. He is also a son who seeks to restore his father's honor by warlike deeds, recapturing land his father had lost. But he embraces a degraded version of the old code, honor at *any* price, as can be shown by an attentive analysis of Hamlet's last soliloquy ("How all occasions do inform against me").

It is, we will see, a speech that reflects not only Hamlet's confusion but also Shakespeare's uncertainty as to how to proceed with a profoundly psychological drama that has not been disentangled from the borrowed melodramatic plot of a revenge play. The most important of the dramatist's solutions to this awkward problem was to delete the whole soliloquy. But, before we turn to the important matter of revision, we must clarify the idea – apparently embraced by Hamlet and accepted at face value by many critics – that he *ought* to revenge his father's murder.

Although Hamlet himself does not tell us this, the play allows us to see that his strong feeling that he ought to kill Claudius for honor's sake is opposed by a contrary feeling that also has moral force, his indirectly admitted aversion to the very code of blood revenge that the Ghost has invoked, a legacy of the medieval chivalric tradition that was fast losing its authority and glamour in Renaissance England. What I think leads Freud and Jones (and many others) astray in addressing this question is their readiness to take at face value Hamlet's belief that he ought to kill Claudius *on the assumption that Shakespeare endorses this view.* Is this the case? We remember Prospero's speech in the last act of *The Tempest:*

> Though with their high wrongs I am struck to the quick,
> Yet with my nobler reason 'gainst my fury
> Do I take part. The rarer action is
> In virtue than in vengeance. 5.1.25-28

I believe Prospero here speaks for Shakespeare. Freud and Jones in particular are prevented from considering this possibility because they are bound by the admittedly tantalizing idea that Hamlet's delay derives from neurotic conflict exposed by "the peculiar nature of his task," the obligation to kill the very man who killed his own father and married his own mother. Whatever this hero's emotional resistance to his task, it cannot be explained by the notion of a defect or flaw in his character. Such description is useful only because an exactly opposite description captures this hero's particular distinction.

Hamlet always confronts his situation and his world directly and with utmost vigor, determined to know the full truth and to set all right. We may call him abnormal only in the sense that he is supernormal, not in any pathological sense. He is, in fact, freer of character weaknesses, of "tragic flaws," than any of the other tragic heroes in the canon. Shakespeare apparently meant to distinguish him in this way, to judge from textual revisions made sometime between the Quarto 2 version of 1604 and the version printed in the Folio after his death. He deleted from Act 1 Horatio's reference to the ominous signs preceding the assassination of Julius Caesar, probably so that Hamlet, also facing a paternalistic tyrant, would not be seen to resemble Brutus. He also deleted the whole passage about "some vicious mole of nature" "in particular men," a passage given heavy emphasis by Laurence Olivier in acknowledged deference to Ernest Jones's Freud-inspired interpretation of the play. My guess is that Shakespeare realized (on reconsideration) that this speech of Hamlet's concerning something like tragic flaws might mislead an audience into thinking that it expressed his own view of the protagonist.

Hamlet's only flaw, one might say (recognizing the fact that his behavior does have some tragic consequences), lies in the very strength of his virtues, strength shown by his uncompromising moral will and his too searching intelligence. From a prudential point of view, his vision is too keen, his noble aspirations impractical. A quick way to gauge the kind of superiority Shakespeare assigns to him is to contrast his words and those of his friend Horatio in this exchange from the Gravedigger's scene:

HAMLET: To what base uses we may return, Horatio! Why may not imagination trace the noble dust of Alexander till 'a find it stopping a bung-hole?

HORATIO: 'Twere to consider too curiously [over-subtly] to consider so.

HAMLET: No, faith, not a jot....

Horatio, sensible and prudent, speaks here for people like ourselves. Risk-defying Hamlet speaks as a hero.

What is the focus of Hamlet's ultra-keen moral vision? It is not only all that is rotten in the state of Denmark but also, and much more radically, the inseparability of death from human existence. The image above all others that audiences of the play remember (and that publicists fairly exploit) is of Hamlet in the Gravedigger's scene holding up and addressing the skull of Yorick.

A father's violent death triggers Hamlet's new awareness of death, which is then heightened by his perception of the warlike footing of the Danish court and of the code of revenge-at-any-cost "when honor's at the stake," embraced by the Ghost, by Laertes, and by Fortinbras. In his zeal to set all right, Hamlet even becomes the unintended agent of death, impulsively killing Polonius whom he mistakes for the king, defensively sending Rosencrantz and Guildenstern, his former school-mates now in the king's employ, to a death intended by Claudius for himself, and, most poignantly, becoming indirectly responsible for the insanity and death of once-loved Ophelia. But the death that pressures him most immediately and inescapably is his own, which he comes to realize is inseparable from the death of the man he is obligated to kill. This blinding insight he discovers in the play's central soliloquy beginning "To be or not to be." He understands there that he must choose between two equally intolerable alternatives. If he does not act, does not kill the king, he is led to endless self-contempt. But if he chooses "to take arms against a sea of troubles," he is led to the realization that killing the king will not after all erase the real source of his anguish, his own consciousness:

> Or to take arms against a sea of troubles,
> And, by opposing, end them. To die, to sleep..,.
> To sleep, perchance to dream. Ay, there's the rub,
> For in that sleep of death what dreams may come
> When we have shuffled off this mortal coil
> Must give us pause.

The idea of killing the king is shown by his associations to be inseparable from the idea of a fearful afterlife for himself. Thus "conscience" [consciousness] "makes a coward" of him, again a victim of endless self-contempt. The soliloquy ends by leaving Hamlet only more deeply aware of his own plight.

Shakespeare has created so searching a psychological drama that he has created for himself, at this midpoint of the play, a very difficult problem – how to work out its resolving action, how to coordinate his extraordinary hero with the crude exigencies of a revenge play. As is well known, *Hamlet* draws upon this popular genre of Elizabethan drama, which included not only Thomas Kyd's *Spanish Tragedy* but also a lost Hamlet play known to scholars as the Ur-Hamlet, said to have been written by Kyd though Shakespeare himself may have had a hand in it. We owe to these sources, for example, the notable addition of a father's ghost. The result is that we have something like two Hamlets jostling along together for several acts – the brilliant hero of consciousness I have been describing and the bloodthirsty avenger. Shakespeare already knows, even before revising his play (as we can see from the unrevised, Quarto 2 version), that his final act will present a modified Hamlet who has worked out for himself a new, albeit incomplete, acceptance of death. What to do, then, with the conventions dictated by the revenge plot, prominent among which is a sufficiently savage slaughter? Harold Bloom comments wittily that "*Hamlet* is Shakespeare's revenge against the revenge play." Indeed, and so, we might ask, how has the playwright managed to achieve that more sophisticated revenge, while accommodating in some way the demands imposed by the play's borrowed framework?

Revision, though it did not *neatly* solve the problem, was crucial to the solutions he worked out. The crisis point, dramaturgically speaking, comes toward the end of Act 4, in the last of the soliloquies, in which Hamlet reproaches himself by seeming to hold up Fortinbras as the exemplar of honorable revenge. I say "seeming" because the soliloquy, though rhetorically brilliant, is at odds with itself, as if Shakespeare was uncertain about where it was leading him, about whether it could be coordinated with the modified Hamlet of the final act.

Let us examine it, keeping in mind the fact that Shakespeare, in the revision indicated by the Folio version, elected to eliminate the entire speech.

> Examples gross as earth exhort me,
> Witness this army of such mass and charge,
> Led by a delicate and tender prince,
> Whose spirit with divine ambition puffed
> Makes mouths at the invisible event,
> Exposing what is mortal and unsure
> To all that fortune, death, and danger dare,
> Even for an eggshell. Rightly to be great
> Is not to stir without great argument,
> But greatly to find quarrel in a straw
> When honour's at the stake. How stand I then

> That have a father killed, a mother stained,
> Excitements of my reason and my blood,
> And let all sleep while, to my shame, I see
> The imminent death of twenty thousand men
> That for a fantasy, a trick of fame,
> Go to their graves like beds, fight for a plot
> Whereon the numbers cannot try the cause
> Which is not tomb enough and continent
> To hide the slain. O, from this time forth
> My thoughts be bloody or be nothing worth.

Although the speech ostensibly holds up Fortinbras as a model, Hamlet's words at the same time tend to subvert the encomium, raising the question whether the young man's ambition has degraded his moral sense. Fortinbras is about to sacrifice the lives of twenty thousand for a plot of ground not worth an eggshell! The three lines beginning "Rightly to be great" are often cited as expressing the code both young men share – *if only another negative word, presumed to be missing, were supplied*. I think the lines make sense as written, and express self-doubt. Hamlet, as I read him, is saying (to himself) that truly noble action requires being stirred by a worthy cause, but Fortinbras finds quarrel in a *straw* and calls that honor! Is it honorable, my doubting Hamlet asks, to lead 20,000 men to their death for this, a "fantasy, a trick of fame"? Does this kind of honor really deserve the name? It may be argued that this reading is negated by Hamlet's *mea culpas* capped by the concluding line in which he resolves to be equally bloodthirsty and ruthless. But Hamlet's fierce self-loathing, here and elsewhere in the play, may be interpreted as showing his *superior moral sense* precisely because it *substitutes* for brutal behavior.

In preparation for Act 5 with its changed Hamlet and the prospect of Fortinbras as Denmark's new leader, Shakespeare apparently thought the character of Fortinbras needed to be reconceived. His revisions of the Quarto 2 text incorporated into the Folio version not only eliminated this entire soliloquy but also added a few lines that make Fortinbras appear more responsible. Another revision softens his view of Laertes (his other so-called foil), making him look more brotherly.

Shakespeare made other changes that smooth the transition to the changed Hamlet of Act 5, deleting two speeches in which he speaks with something like glee about the fate of Rosencrantz and Guildenstern and with something like brutality to his mother. In Act 5 he added lines that justify the removal of Claudius in Christian rather than honor-bound chivalric terms. And he altered one memorable passage to imply that Hamlet, in his resignation or fatalism (for he continues to associate the king's death with his own), is no longer troubled by the fear of something after death. Quarto 2 reads: "Since no man of aught he leaves, knows, what is't to leave betimes. Let be." In the Folio version we read: "Since no man has aught of what he leaves, what is't to leave betimes." Not only is the revised version more clearly worded but it changes the idea of not *knowing* what one leaves (closer to the language of Montaigne that it borrows) to not *having* what one leaves, and drops the "let be," yielding a more Christian picture of the hero in his preparation for death.

These textual changes have become a nuisance for editors and critics. Most in fact have not really accepted the major deletions. (The Norton Shakespeare, for example, trying to be both faithful to Shakespeare and accommodating to the reader who should not be deprived of memorable language, italicizes these passages without removing them.) The awkward but inescapable fact is that the texts we are most familiar with, in classrooms and elsewhere, are hybrids. This substantial textual problem must restrain any critic's ambition to discover the overall coherence of the play. And it will always provide support for T. S. Eliot's sour judgment that *Hamlet* is an artistic failure. But the revisions also help to clarify our understanding of the important modifications in Act 5.

Shakespeare has taken some trouble to prepare us for a modified Hamlet. A basic shift in the hero's outlook is indicated in both texts by the sea voyage that takes place off stage, and is reported for us by Horatio who reads Hamlet's description of the incident, which involves cunning counterplotting against Claudius. The Prince's artful maneuver implies a less brooding, more resourceful young man. There is a difference, after all, between his earlier, impulsive stabbing of Polonius and his present action against the two who are doing the king's dirty work, which requires forging a new letter and the fore-thoughtful possession of his father's seal. It is clearly a more confident and bolder Hamlet who then takes advantage of an encounter with pirates to board their ship and bargain with them for a return to Denmark. The whole recounted episode becomes symbolically suggestive when we hear the returned Hamlet assert, in his first exchange with King Claudius, "This is I, Hamlet the Dane," signaling to one and all that he is no longer the son, that he is taking his father's place. Tellingly, we hear no more from or about the Ghost in Act 5.

The change in Hamlet is, of course, not a complete transformation. A certain fatalism, a sense of death's nearness, remains, though accompanied now by a new readiness, and with Christian consolation replacing the warrior's contempt for cowardice. Speaking to Horatio, Hamlet finds reassurance in "a divinity that shapes our ends" but not without adding "Rough-hew them how we will." He now says, alluding to Matthew, "There's a special Providence in the fall of a sparrow," but follows this immediately with the fatalistic "If it be now, 'tis not to come, if it be not to come, it will be now; if it be not now yet it will come. The readiness is all." He accepts with composure and even confidence the King's wager on him in a duel with Laertes, before adding "But thou wouldst not think how ill all's here about my heart," the hard-to-pronounce phrasing drawing out his anxiety. Prudent Horatio advises him not to proceed with the duel, advice that Hamlet heroically disdains with the phrase "We defy augury." And he does not in fact lose the duel but is fatally wounded by an illegal thrust from a poisoned rapier, brought down not by hubris but by a residue of his old innocence, as the cunning Claudius foresaw when he told Laertes that Hamlet is free from contriving and will not peruse the foils.

Smitten as they were by the oedipal scenario, Freud and Jones paid no attention to Act 5, nor could they have found there further support for it. They might, of course, have turned to another scenario familiar to psychoanalysis, the story of a young man who has over time gained enough maturity to replace a father-figure by socially acceptable means rather than by violence – something like what the psychoanalyst Ernst Kris did successfully in writing about "Prince Hal's Conflict." But Prince Hamlet is no Prince Hal. Too much has happened, he has seen too deeply into existence and its penumbra of death. His story cannot be a romance or a *bildungsroman*. It must be a tragedy.

The playwright's difficult final task was to work out a denouement for his extensive modification of the revenge play that still allows the destruction of the villain to be accomplished with satisfying savagery. His artful melding of the two Hamlets enables the avenger to kill the villain fiercely but only when he understands not only how dishonorably he has been set up but also that he himself is already mortally wounded. Hamlet does not escape, in other words, his earlier dark knowledge that the king's death entails his own.

True to the tradition of tragic denouements, a measure of order is finally restored, its restoration (with a "revised" Fortinbras in charge) authorized by the dying hero. But the eulogy pronounced on his death by his friend Horatio only outlines the circumstances of the action we have witnessed, quite missing the complexities of motivation, the inner drama that this essay has attempted to deal with. This may be Shakespeare's way of saying that, in a profound tragedy, there can be no final, readily describable moral significance, that the meaning of what we have witnessed must belong, in part, to mystery.

Georg Brandes and Sigmund Freud: Good Europeans

(Author's Note. This essay originally contained as many pages of endnotes as of text. My current judgment is that these notes are best omitted altogether. Little or nothing in the text calls out for supporting evidence. It offers a view of Freud as a man in his European setting rather than as a shaper of modern thought.)

When the influential and talented Danish critic Georg Brandes discovered the work of Friedrich Nietzsche and wrote the philosopher an admiring letter, he received this reply: "It gives me great joy that such a good European and cultural missionary as yourself wishes to be counted among [my faithful few readers], and I want to thank you most gratefully for this welcome intention." By "good European," a phrase he had used in several books, Nietzsche meant to highlight two features of an ideal type: a European intellectual who had the range and independence to free himself from narrowly nationalistic loyalties; and one whose "will to truth" was strong enough to put aside the prevailing morality based on the idea of divine guidance and develop a new one whose aim was primarily to foster the production of great individuals.

Brandes' six-volume study, *Main Currents in European Literature*, his comprehensive portraits of such universal cultural figures as Michelangelo, Shakespeare, Voltaire and Goethe, and his essays on Scandinavian and Eastern European writers are indeed far ranging, freshly thought out and charged with feeling. Brandes rapidly mastered the languages and read widely in the literatures of France, Germany and Britain, even while remaining deeply attached to his native tongue. (A great sorrow of his life was that the Danish language he especially loved to use could not be understood by most of his readers and audiences.) By 1864, at the age of twenty-two, he had already won a reputation as an eloquent and vehement fighter against religious and political conservatism in Denmark, attacking a book whose timid argument was that "our old faith" could not be affected by Darwin's new biological science. For *this* critic, truth was not so negotiable, and his bold language soon attracted the attention of no less a cultural fighter than Henrik Ibsen, fourteen years older, who hailed the young man as an intellectual emancipator, an ally in the "work of bringing about a much needed revolution of the human spirit." By the time he was thirty, Brandes was lecturing to audiences across the continent, delighting them with his vivacity, clarity, incisiveness, and charm, while at the same time scolding their mediocrity, for which his favorite synonym was stupidity. One auditor named Sigmund Freud heard him lecture in Vienna in 1900 and was surprised and a bit impressed as well by the lecturer's daring to insult his conventionally minded audience.

Trying to label himself, Brandes judged that "philosopher is too big a word and critic too small." He is best described as a kind of cultural inspirer. Ibsen admired his "feeling for the future"; Edmund Gosse in England admired his ability to "awaken 'ecstasy' in others." Like Freud, he was not really a reformer seeking change by political means. (The French statesman Georges Clemenceau praised him in 1904 as "a European in the largest and most noble sense of the word," but his admiration turned to scorn during the Great War when his hero emerged as a fierce pacifist.) Although both Brandes and Freud, critics of their constricted societies, stoutly welcomed more freedom, neither put much stock in political reforms: they were aiming at a more radical change of feeling and thought.

Freud too was a "good European." Though more rooted in Vienna than Brandes was in Copenhagen and more resistant to removing himself from his home country, he never quite felt himself to be an Austrian national, taking a dim view of the Viennese bourgeoisie in general and of the Viennese medical establishment in particular. What remained of his national loyalty was further eroded by the breakup of the Austro-Hungarian empire in 1918 and then destroyed by the Nazis when they swallowed Austria and drove its Jews to exile or extinction. Back in the 1880s, during his Paris years, Freud explained to a French physician who thirsted for revenge against Germany that he was a Jew and thus neither Austrian nor German. Brandes made a similar remark: "In terms of nationality I should always be a foreigner [because of my Jewishness]. I was, however, born in Denmark of Danish parents." Highly cultured Jews like Brandes and Freud are, perhaps ironically, excellent candidates for Nietzsche's ideal type because anti-Semitic prejudice helped to make them instinctive internationalists and moral combatants. Freud's will to truth, embodied in psychoanalysis, was a subtler moral vehicle than any Brandes could wield, but the moral imperative in the thinking of both was linked to a deep respect for the primary importance of human psychology.

The political and religious views of the two men were similar. Freud called himself "a liberal of the old school," favoring more personal freedom but skeptical about egalitarian democracy and, despite his dissatisfaction with the existing economic system, repelled by the communist experiment in Soviet Russia. Both he and Brandes endeavored to educate others but were not very hopeful about the results. Brandes told a feminist friend that he was not truly a democrat because he feared majorities, yet he admitted that there was probably no better system than democracy to insure against the capriciousness of monarchy and oligarchy. Freud off the record admitted that he found most people "worthless," "a wretched lot," "nuisances to themselves and others," although he reached out famously if not always very hopefully to that large group of "nuisances" he called neurotics. With Dr. Stockmann, Ibsen's "enemy of the people," these men knew that, to achieve moral progress, opposition to the status quo would always be required because the status quo would always be defended by the majority, the "compact majority."

Like Nietzsche, Brandes and Freud perceived religion in its customary forms as a stumbling block to the advance of civilization. Each has with some justification been labeled an atheist, but that word can be misleading in light of the fact that they were intellectual Jews. Like many in that group, they were not interested in theology or the question of divine existence. (Freud remarked tartly: "I believe that one day metaphysics will be condemned as a nuisance, as a survival of the period of religious *Weltanschauung*.") But a sense of Jewish identity for both was unequivocal, and it was strengthened, not weakened, by the anti-Semitism that surrounded them. Their Jewishness prepared them to be in the opposition and fortified their defiant courage about truth.

Brandes and Freud are also linked, with each other and with Nietzsche, by their consistent and conspicuous psychological approach to cultural topics. Freud's commitment in this regard requires no emphasis. Brandes embraced a similar commitment, expressing it like a credo in his doctoral dissertation (as later described in his autobiography) and in the opening pages of the book that established his reputation, the first volume of *Main Currents in Nineteenth Century Literature*. "My conviction grew," he reminisced in the former, "that all profound historical research is psychical research [because the fundamental question for the critic of any art or philosophy] is the nature of the producing mind from which it springs." "Literary criticism," he wrote in the latter, "is, in its profoundest significance, psychology, the study of the history of the soul." Brandes' formative thinking evolved from an early immersion in philosophy (Kierkegaard, Hegel, Feuerbach) to the quasi-scientific literary criticism of Taine, his first real mentor in the work of his maturity. But he came to feel that Taine's approach led in practice toward abstraction, toward seeing individual writers as types rather than as idiosyncratic geniuses. Rejecting Taine's claim that "Science is going to tackle the human soul," Brandes declared: "The kernel of my work was a protest against this theory." His lasting model proved to be Sainte-Beuve, whose distinction as a critic was an ability "to understand and interpret a great number of other minds."

The *careers* of these two near contemporaries also contain a number of striking similarities. The destination of each man's first important trip abroad was Paris where a professional role model awaited (Taine for Brandes, Charcot for Freud), some of whose work each thereupon translated into his native language. Each man early on was attracted to the work of John Stuart Mill and translated some his work as well. Each sought vainly over many years to receive a professorial appointment, less out of respect for academicians than for income and public respect; each was denied, largely for the same reason, anti-Semitism; and each finally attained this coveted goal in middle age (Freud at 46, Brandes at 60). Each man made one long-wished-for trip to the ancient Acropolis, that symbolic peak of European culture, and each was overcome with emotion, adducing similar reasons. Brandes said: "I have not been able to manage this trip before now; I am 80 years old and have finally achieved it." Freud looked back in 1936 to a trip made in 1904 and analyzed the uneasiness he felt in fulfilling a wish that had long seemed out of reach, its fulfillment too good to be true. He realized that his satisfaction was blocked by "filial piety," by guilt at having surpassed his uneducated father, as if he were forbidden to do so, and concluded that this uneasiness "comes back to me now that I myself have grown old and stand in need of forbearance and can travel no more."

Another notable likeness between them was their more than rational fascination with certain world-historical figures. The fascination was based in part, of course, on their understanding that such men transcend as well as represent their age, and will never be surpassed. But it was also a bit over the mark, suggesting a kind of covert personal identification. Although always well informed, Brandes' enthusiasms were not free of rhetorical excess, and Freud took liberties with the historical record to endorse the

Oxfordian theory of Shakespearean authorship and the Egyptian identity of Moses.

Yet another link is that each man made one lecture trip to America, Freud in 1909, Brandes in 1914, and each found it a disagreeable place – crude and incoherent, in a word uncultured. In this mutual distaste, we might say that they were good Europeans in an ironic sense, contemptuous about the New World despite their progressive outlook in most respects. In 1921 Brandes told a *New York Times* reporter, in dismay and disgust, that Europe is finished and the age of American domination (that is, of money worship and cultural mediocrity) has begun. The country hails liberty, he added, but "the liberty closest to the heart of an American is the liberty to acquire." Freud's anti-Americanism was also harsh and peculiarly petulant. He persisted after his visit in calling every abdominal discomfort "American colitis." He told his future biographer Ernest Jones, "America is a mistake, a gigantic mistake, it is true, but still a mistake." Jones could only offer in defense of his hero the judgment that "he was a good European, with a sense of dignity and a respect for learning, not prominent then in America." But at the end of his life, when Freud could not help realizing that the future of his beloved child, psychoanalysis, lay not in continental Europe but in England and, inevitably, in America, he softened this prejudicial view. "America," he wrote in a letter of March 1939, "seems to me an anti-Paradise, but it has so much space and so many possibilities and ultimately one does come to belong there. Einstein told a visitor recently that at first America seemed like a caricature of a country to him, but that now he feels quite at home there."

A final similarity between the two careers is that in about the same year, when Brandes was about 80 and Freud about 70, each wrote his first and only book-length attack on religious belief, one titled *Jesus, A Myth* and the other *The Future of An Illusion*. Though offended by modern theism, neither quite dismissed it, unlike today's fiery, articulate atheists (Richard Dawkins, Daniel Dennett, Sam Harris, Christopher Hitchens), because they knew how deeply religious belief was involved in the history and psychology of mankind. The persisting human attachment to retrograde beliefs had to be analyzed, explained, and, with a sense of resignation, in view of the stubborn mediocrity of the human animal, accepted.

Famous for much of their long lives, Brandes and Freud inevitably knew of one another's existence, but were only slightly familiar with one another's work. Freud had attended a Brandes lecture, had consulted his pages on *Hamlet* in forming his own view of the play, and had read through one of his books, *Moderne Geister*, which he didn't much like, mainly because it approved of Mill's too liberal views on women. On this topic Freud was old-fashioned, remarking that Mill "lacked a sense of the absurd" when he said that women could and should compete with men in the workplace. "We surely agree that the management of a house and children requires the whole of a human being....Nature has determined women's destiny." Brandes had a regressive side too, grumbling that "there was nothing to be had from dreams," citing as proof that he had dreamed twice he was a woman! He later told his secretary that Freud's theories like the Oedipus complex were "disgusting, and may be left to America where they are said to be very successful." One would not expect the two to hit it off if they were ever to meet for private conversation. But they did meet once for this purpose toward the end of their lives, and the meeting was memorable for both.

In the spring of 1925, Brandes was again lecturing in Vienna, and Freud took the trouble to visit him at his hotel. Brandes thereupon reported to his secretary, "I have just had an interesting visitor – Freud! There's a great man. Meeting him is an experience." After a pause he added, "Freud paid me the greatest compliment I have ever received – he said I reminded him of the prophet Isaiah, the prophet most dear to my heart.... How seldom one meets a man who can teach one something." His secretary further reported that, a few months later, on his seventieth birthday, he singled out from some congratulatory letters one from Freud, his new friend, that particularly pleased him. It is heartening to learn of this late and warm encounter between two intellectual warriors who had accomplished so much in their lives to earn the Nietzschean accolade of good European.

The Value of Freud's Psychoanalysis Today

The high reputation of psychoanalysis in the 1940s and 1950s was in large part based on its claim of therapeutic efficacy. Over the subsequent decades this claim lost much of its strength. Many former analysands (among whom I am one) would agree that they did indeed learn something about themselves and, as advertised, have never forgotten what they learned. But not many would also say that this education resulted in a significant change of character, a significant gain in the kind of inner freedom that their analysts would call autonomy. Some would add that the experience has enabled them to allay their disappointments with a sense of humor about themselves. But to be able to smile ruefully at the regular recurrence of familiar defensive maneuvers seems a small gain after all. We all learn from life experience, of course, and become wiser about our abilities, our place in the world and our relations with other people, but, again, that doesn't much alter those stubborn unconscious determinants. The best summary of the matter, in my view, was offered by one candid psychoanalyst: "by the age of 6 you've had it." The same thought was expressed with fine pathos by the poet Philip Larkin: "An only life can take so long to climb/ Clear of its wrong beginnings, and may never."

This, however, is not quite all that needs to be said about the value of psychoanalysis today. And, perhaps not surprisingly, it is Freud himself who points us in a further direction. He offered this valuable hint to the poet Hilda Doolittle (known as H.D.), whom he talked to (one can hardly say "analyzed") for some months in the last years of his life. "My discoveries," he told her, "are not primarily a heal-all. My discoveries are a basis for a very grave philosophy. There are very few who understand this, there are very few who are capable of understanding this." (H.D., *Tribute to Freud*, 1956, p. 25.)

This somber assessment turns our attention away from the hopeless dream of a cure, and redirects it to improving our understanding of human nature itself. That is to say, the personal insight gained in a psychoanalysis acquires strength and importance when it engages our intellect and imagination in a wider arc of understanding. Shifting our goal from healing to understanding, and widening the object to be understood from self to human nature, puts the mind hampered and discouraged by neurosis to active and rewarding work.

Basically what one learns from psychoanalytic therapy is something about the complex interaction in one's own mind between desires and fears, an interaction made fiendishly subtle by the fact that these elements are more or less unconscious, only indirectly and imperfectly available to one's understanding and not readily acceptable when they are better understood. The bigger picture that confronts us when we consider other minds as well, noticing what others think about themselves and about one another, is easier to read. About the great buzz of psychological description all around us, we cannot help noticing how commonly these descriptions are stamped and vitiated by moral judgments, and thus almost appeal for interpretation. People tend to see and judge themselves and one another simply as good or bad, innocent or guilty, correct (one of us) or confused (one of them). Political and religious judgments are particularly characterized by this polarizing tendency.

Despite his primary emphasis on individual psychology, it is again Freud who shows us how we can make use of this polarizing tendency to gain insight into human nature itself. In "Thoughts for the Times on War and Death" (1915), commenting on human nature in light of the terrible, disillusioning war in which Europe was engaged, he analyzed with powerful irony the moral misjudgments which this extreme situation exposed. The analysis is encapsulated in one sentence: "In reality our fellow-citizens have not sunk so low as we feared because they had never risen so high as we believed." That is to say, human beings are both better and worse than they think they are. They are better because they typically judge themselves bad or sinful merely because they have bad thoughts or feelings. Freud made clear that, in the light of his discoveries of infantile conflicts and their consequences, we are not responsible for these thoughts or feelings in themselves, only for the way we act upon them with the help of our adult judgment. The fact that we are often able to refrain from acting on them testifies to the presence of a working moral sense. At the same time we are worse than we think we are because we often deny even the presence of those "bad" thoughts and feelings, doing so every time we think of ourselves as simply good or innocent. Conscience, whatever moralists say, he knew to be a peculiarly flexible faculty, allowing many to permit themselves anti-social actions and, at the same time, to condemn themselves excessively with a sense of guilt for mere thoughts or small infractions. Even for the "analyzed" among us, self-knowledge is not always secure and strong enough to protect us from making these simplified judgments about others and about ourselves.

Achieving self-knowledge has, of course, been the central goal of moral philosophy from Plato to Freud. None of the major writers in this tradition believed this task would be easy. We remember Plato's myth of the cave, which pictures the human mind as a place where images of truth are reflected by firelight and are mistaken for the full truth, symbolized by the light of the sun. We remember Spinoza's admonition, at the end of his ambitious *Ethics*, that self-knowledge cannot be discovered "without great labor...but all noble things are as difficult as they are rare." Then there is Kant's reminder that our all-important freedom as moral agents must be understood as limited by the determining constraints of nature's laws. And there is Schopenhauer's stubborn pessimism based on the assumption of an omnipresent unconscious will. And Nietzsche's exceedingly strenuous summons to self-overcoming. A new difficulty is added to these already difficult teachings by Freud's "grave philosophy." Given the fact that our very imperfectly understood infantile conflicts exert so much influence on our adult character, it becomes impossible beyond a point to follow the Socratic dictum: Know Thyself.

It is to this philosophical tradition that Freud's ethical teachings belong, as well as to psychological science. The place of his psychoanalysis in this tradition has been effectively explored in recent years by writers trained in moral philosophy as well as in psychoanalysis, among whom I will name again Alfred Tauber (*Freud: the Reluctant Philosopher*), Marcia Cavell (*Becoming a Subject: Reflections in Philosophy and Psychoanalysis*) and Jonathan Lear (*Love and Its Place in Nature: A Philosophical Interpretation of Freudian Psychoanalysis*). Combining what we can learn from psychoanalysis, as readers or patients, with what we can learn from moral philosophy makes the Freudian contribution to this tradition especially rich.

I want to conclude on a hopeful note. A peculiar feature of psychoanalytic therapy is that it does not really end when the formal sessions between doctor and patient come to end. For the patient, the mental activity known as "working through" has been set in motion and lasts a lifetime. What one learns every day just from living a life is always intermixed with what one has learned about one's more or less hidden self. The process often reminds me of John Dewey's remark, "Education is not a preparation for life, education *is* life." Some former patients, I know, find this ongoing aspect of "working through" burdensome, and complain that psychoanalysis "never lets you go." But I am inclined to find the experience advantageous on the whole. It enables me to think of the life I am living as *necessarily* incomplete and unfinished. Our lives, after all, are not works of narrative art, shaped by some sort of fitting closure. And of course they are not preludes to any other life.

But these pages, dear Reader, constitute a text, and so may be brought to a formal conclusion.

Singular Time:
Three Freudian Essentials

Camelia Elias

Storytelling

In his new book, *Freud: Some Literary Perspectives*, David Gordon elegantly makes the apt observation that Freud thought of his discoveries not so much as science but more as philosophy; a philosophy of life and experience in general. The invitation is thus to appreciate the poetry of psychoanalysis and the poetics of experiencing a life's event through psychoanalysis, insofar as psychoanalysis relates to an act of seeking to know different facets of ourselves. We know what there is to know about ourselves in context, and to the extent that culture allows us to know something about ourselves – when it downright won't dictate what we 'ought' to know about ourselves, because that's what culture does best, dictate – but what about the rest?

Any one significant event in our lives that we seek to 'work through', either by getting to know its details, understanding it, or accepting it, involves a continuous process. In most critical studies Freud is referred to as a structuralist, belonging to the school of thought that maintains a belief in language as a binary experience that goes something along these lines: If you understand that you are a man, you do so because you are not a woman. If you feel disconnected in life, it's a good idea to reconstruct the events in your life that have contributed to that disconnect, and start getting a sense of what it means to be whole again. All very neat, but as Freud has demonstrated, if there is anything worth appreciating, then it is the very ambiguity of life. How does a transgender subject reconstruct his or her wholeness, when there isn't one there to begin with? And if there is one, where do we locate it? In the mother's womb? At the infant, solipsistic stage? What is the story here?

Gordon ends his book here with a citation that I find relevant in assessing what is the most important aspect in reading Freud, namely the idea of psychoanalysis as storytelling. He references Freud telling his friend, the poet H.D. the following: "My discoveries are not primarily a heal-all. My discoveries are a basis for a very grave philosophy. There are very few who understand this, there are very few who are capable of understanding this"[1] (p. 92). Gordon extrapolates from this the understanding that what one gains from psychoanalysis is the knowledge about the value of the mind's interaction between desires and fears. I see this as an interaction that not only embodies, but is also enabled by the kind of stories we end up telling ourselves. Says Gordon:

> The personal insight gained in a psychoanalysis acquires strength and importance when it engages our intellect and imagination in a wider arc of understanding. Shifting our goal from healing to understanding, and widening the object to be understood from

---

[1] H.D., *Tribute to Freud,* 1956 (New York: New Directions Books), p. 25

> self to human nature, puts the mind hampered and discouraged by neurosis to active and rewarding work (p. 92).

Indeed, imagination itself can be said to have a wider scope than our aims at integration: mind with body, psyche with soul, and so on. Here, in my own understanding of Freud's writings I have come to the realization that Freud uses the psyche as a tool for divination about one's life: you ask the psyche a question, and out pops an answer. The psyche itself is an oracle. This idea is supported by Freud's own life long interest in myth, and his fascination with all types of oracles, the oracle at Delphi *par excellence.*

As oracles facilitate getting a glimpse into ourselves, a strange and ambiguous prophetic line about the course of our lives can completely derail the course we are on to begin with. In this sense oracles instigate to action. "You will kill your father," the Pythia said to Oedipus, and off he went to participate in the creation of his own story. Oedipus took the unreality of the situation at the time of the prophecy and turned into reality. We can only imagine what might have happened if Oedipus had stayed at home ignoring the fated words, instead of running away from fear. But that would not have been a good story.

It is my contention that much of Freud's writing suggests that what we can use the psyche for, apart from 'working through', is to make poetry of our lives: Beautiful, sublime, and tragic poetry; useful too, as some of the poetic lines we can arrive at, after having experienced some tremendous events, can lead precisely to an appreciation of life in its simplest form, namely, the form which reduces range to universality, or rather, which brings the individual range of our capacity to experience to a universal state of understanding the implications of 'Know thyself'.

Sometimes I'm tempted to replace Freud's word 'discovery' with 'storytelling' every time I stumble on it. There are many possibilities.

Time

It is commonly acknowledged by anyone who has ever written a single line on Freud that what Freud wanted above all was to be useful. In all of his social and private functions, Freud wanted to be useful. In this sense he was a great teacher. Perhaps intuitively Freud had a good grasp of the wisdom triad: understand, accept, and let go. For Oedipus, the implication of the oracle at Delphi must have resonated in this way: 'Understand that you must kill your father. Accept the event. Get on with the program.' But Oedipus was not riding that wave of catching the finer point, or print. He was not in the oracular, so to speak. Oedipus must have thought, 'I must do something before the time comes. The dreadful time. I must act.'

One of the good things here, and that we can appreciate, is that Oedipus did not suffer from a midlife crisis. He didn't spend time, like most us do if we care to know ourselves, with the fundamental question: 'What am I afraid of?' Oedipus knew exactly what he feared and he acted accordingly. His life had a purpose. Except for the guilt part. Nowhere does the oracle say, 'and thou shalt feel guilty afterwards', but Oedipus interpreted it that way. So his actions against the oracle were based on the unreality of guilt, on anticipation.

Historically, the people who were most obsessed with integration must have been the alchemists of the Renaissance time: 'Integrate your opposites, and let your magic glitter.' I am seduced by this idea, as I think Freud was too. But how to go about it? Logically speaking, for any integration of parts to occur, one must have them, the parts, that is. Psychoanalytically speaking, what we are 'working through' often relates to how we must make our cuts accordingly. Cut to the essentials.

An interesting woodcut[2] from 1482 depicts Zeus as he is 'working on' the process of unmanning his father, Saturn. This is the story of repeated fatherhood acts and the beginning of the story of 'working through', as Saturn in his own time did the same to his father, Uranus.

2   *The unmanning of Saturn.* Medieval woodcut. HENKEL, M.D. (1922). De houtsneden van Mansion's 'Ovide Moralisé'. (Bruges 1484, Uitg. Kon. Oudheidkundig Genootschap, P.N. van Kampen & Zoon, Amsterdam.)

Most would see this as an act of castration that perpetuates itself through time – the cutting of the man's essentials in a sacrificing ritual – but a closer look at what happens here indicates that what we are dealing with is perhaps a process of cutting TO the essentials. As Saturn holds into his right hand both the scythe and the ouroboros, symbols of purging and continuity, he indicates that he holds the power over knowing what's essential. Time and continuity as represented by the ouroboros work hand in hand with the cutting blade. Continuity is only possible insofar as there is repetition of the same. All that which is completed and outdated must be cut. In his left hand Saturn holds a child. Nothing protects his genitals. The grown son is free to do what he must. Zeus's mother witnesses the act impassively, while his love interest plays the tambourine naked. I don't detect much guilt here. While the blood sprouts out of Saturn's cut limb, disclosing a hole, we are meant to think of time as always ritualistic. In sacred space, whatever we do is justified and necessary. I still don't see how guilt would feature here. What did the alchemists know? What did Freud know, but didn't say?

As *The Odyssey* teaches us, the fathers are both fathers of gods and men and also sons. Athena participates in the creation of a story of ambiguity, when she states: "Father, son of Cronos, king of kings..."[3] Zeus, too is both the father of gods and men, and the son of Cronos, or Saturn. We are not allowed to contemplate too much the law of non-contradiction – either you are a god, or you are not – as we accept at face value the idea that gods are men of action, and because of that they must pay with emasculation for having fathered sons. Freud was not so interested in

---

3 Homer, *The Odyssey*. Trans. Charles Stein (Berkeley, CA: North Atlantic Books, c2008), p. 15.

the women's role in this whole process, except perhaps to suggest that the woman, as the mother of sons who castrate their fathers, teaches men something about the value of detachment.

Solipsism

What we find at the core of psychoanalysis is the idea that, logically speaking, it is impossible to feel depressed or alone if you choose to communicate. The implicit emotional message here must be the following: 'Be vulnerable, keep talking about it, and you'll be fine.' However, in terms of the content that appeals to reason here, as this addresses the ambivalent subject who, by virtue of being ambivalent is already IN communication, one must wonder what we can make of the individual, solipsistic experience of a repeated act. What does patricide mean?

In "Totem and Taboo" Freud conjectures that the first act of patricide must have left an indelible mark on our humanity. What we cannot erase at the physical level of execution becomes part of the collective obsession with the intention to execute (a murder, desire, fear, sex). By way of quoting the literary titan, Goethe, Freud concludes his essay with these lines:

> Neurotics are above all *inhibited* in their actions: with them the thought is a complete substitute for the deed. Primitive men, on the other hand, are *uninhibited:* thought passes directly into action. With them it is rather the deed that is a substitute for the thought. And that is why, without laying claim to any finality of judgment, I think that in the case before us it may safely be assumed that 'in the beginning was the Deed'.[4]

---

4 "Totem and Taboo." *The Freud Reader.* Ed. Peter Gray. (New York: W.W. Norton & Company, 1989), p. 513.

What Freud identifies here, albeit obliquely, is idea that what separates intention from action is basically nothing. Perhaps we can lump together the inhibited with the uninhibited in the figure of the true solipsist, and then make the following assumptions:

Firstly, a solipsist will never experience the need to communicate anything whatsoever, least of all his thoughts – so the advice above, 'be vulnerable' is bound to be an exercise in futility. The solipsist's impossibility to communicate has at least two reasons: 1) he doesn't know the meaning of being dependent on others, 2) nor is he possessive. A solipsist's discourse is never marked by the signs of constant claiming and clamoring: You will never hear a solipsist say: "It's mine," whether relating to objects or people. Nor will he demand: "Give me some attention, now."

Secondly, logically speaking you cannot pair solipsism with a conditional – 'IF you choose to communicate, you'll fix your bruised ego.' A true solipsist either kills his father or he doesn't. As the solipsist is neither a neurotic, nor a primitive man, he realizes that guilt eschews our understanding of death as the most limiting of experiences. So he won't feel any. In this sense, the solipsist is always the embodiment of the condition of IS, and never of IF (and even 'as if', or 'maybe').

Thirdly, logically speaking the solipsist doesn't make any sense, as he also embodies a contradiction in terms: he exists in spite of annihilating his existence through thinking of the inconvenience of having been born, and acting thereupon (often by killing his father).

As much as Freud wanted to move in deliberate, steady, and predictable moves in his psychoanalytic discoveries, he also realized that there isn't really anything that separates the problem of knowing from the problem of acting, and that this non-separation is precisely what constitutes the realm of the imagination and of literature. Unlike others who have identified solipsism with a moral impasse[5], Freud understood that solipsism ultimately has to do with how we get to honor our common sense by acknowledging the power of ambiguity in all our life experiences. On this he says:

> Consciousness makes each of us aware only of his own states of mind; that other people, too, possess a consciousness is an inference which we draw by analogy from their observable utterances and actions, in order to make this behavior of theirs intelligible to us. (It would no doubt be psychologically more correct to put it in this way: that without any special reflection we attribute to everyone else our own constitution and therefore our consciousness as well, and that this identification is a sine qua non of understanding) [...] Psycho-analysis demands nothing more than that we should apply this process of inference to ourselves also – a proceeding to which, it is true, we are not constitutionally inclined. If we do this, we must say: all the acts and manifestations which I notice in myself and do not know how to link up with the rest of my mental life must be judged *as if they belonged to someone else:* they are to be explained by a mental life ascribed to this other person (*The Freud Reader,* 575-576; my emphasis).

Freud thus understood that the reason why good storytelling makes sense is because most subjects realize that they live in a world of fantasies. Two fantasies, to be more precise: the fantasy

---

[5] See, Harold Kaplan's *The Solipsism of Modern Fiction: Comedy, Tragedy, and Heroism* (Ohio University Press, 1966), and Betty Friedan's *The Feminine Mystique,* where she engages directly with what she calls Freud's sexual solipsism (New York: W.W. Norton, 1963).

of fantasy and the fantasy of reality. In this sense, and psychologically speaking, Oedipus has a point. When he leaves home out of the fear that he might commit murder if he stays, what he embarks on is the serpent's path, the path of passing. The ouroboros, the serpent that eats its own tail, is Oedipus's *rendez-vous* with time, where he meets his 'other' self, the murderous self that he has been imagining ever since the oracle. When the time is right, and while passing the time, Oedipus then goes on to execute 'the Deed': the unintended murder of his father. But does this 'non-intention' fix his existential problem? It doesn't. What it does is teach us the lesson of resistance. 'What you fear, you don't escape', popular wisdom has it, and it makes us pay attention to new trends in psychology and how they relate to the stories of the self as they are made up in time.

Cognitive psychology, as against Freudian psychology – or the change of attitude vs. the talking cure philosophy – claims to have come up with some efficient remedies against the wounds in the soul. Its reductive methods, however, help only the uninhibited, or those who are not accustomed to thinking too much. The ones into the habit of breathing, of bringing their awareness close to the blade in Saturn's scythe may reflect on what another literary titan, Emile Cioran, said: "You cannot protect your solitude if you cannot make yourself odious."[6]

What psychoanalysis in literary perspectives demonstrates is that obsessions must not be vanquished, but completed. Stories unfold in time; the time we take to think about how we can know ourselves better; the time it takes to think of alternative selves, or to think of magical solutions to real problems; the time it takes

---

6 *All Gall is Divided. Gnomes and Apothegms.* (Trans. Richard Howard. New York: Arcade, 1999), p. 69.

to imagine ourselves without a self, or with that of an other. 'I' as my mother. I am tempted to say that perhaps women make better fathers. But let that be the topic of another essay.

Meanwhile, my closing comment here, by drawing on three Freudian concepts that are not always discussed from the point of view of associative thinking as it relies on a system of tight methodology, is to suggest that storytelling, time, and solipsism function as a gate to using the psyche in creative way. In a literary perspective, as the psyche itself can be seen as a storytelling machine, by permuting with its images, symbols, latent and non-manifest content, we can draw on its power whenever we engage in the act of interpreting a text. Perhaps the art is to start with the blind spot, even before we realize that there is one there. Perhaps this is what Freud knew, namely, that by surrendering to the flow of events, to the reading of omens rather than trying to control them, we get a glimpse into how we can turn our sense of 'waiting for it to happen' into a type of communication that honors its 'other' premise: 'know thyself, so that you can know thy place.'

About the Author

David Gordon is Emeritus Professor of English at Hunter College and the Graduate School of the City University of New York. Among his books are *D.H. Lawrence as a Literary Critic, Literary Art and the Unconscious, Iris Murdoch's Fables of Unselfing and Seven Literary Antitheists from Diderot to Beckett,* the last also published by EyeCorner Press.